Karaoke Nights

ETHNOGRAPHIC ALTERNATIVES BOOK SERIES

Series Editor
Carolyn Ellis
Arthur P. Bochner
(both at the University of South Florida)

About the Series:

Ethnographic Alternatives emphasizes experimental forms of qualitative writing that blur the boundaries between social sciences and humanities. The editors encourage submissions that experiment with novel forms of expressing lived experience, including literary, poetic, autobiographical, multi-voiced, conversational, critical, visual, performative, and co-constructed representations. Emphasis should be on expressing concrete lived experience through narrative modes of writing.

We are interested in ethnographic alternatives that promote narration of local stories; literary modes of descriptive scene setting, dialogue, and unfolding action; and inclusion of the author's subjective reactions, involvement in the research process, and strategies for practicing reflexive fieldwork.

Please send proposals to:

Carolyn Ellis and Arthur P. Bochner
College of Arts and Sciences
Department of Communication
University of South Florida
4202 East Fowler Avenue, CIS 1040
Tampa, FL 33620-7800
Email: cellis@chuma.cas.usf.edu

Books in the Series:

Volume 1, *Composing Ethnography: Alternative Forms of Qualitative Writing*, Carolyn Ellis and Arthur P. Bochner, editors

Volume 2, *Opportunity House: Ethnographic Stories of Mental Retardation*, Michael V. Angrosino

Volume 3, *Kaleidoscope Notes: Writing Women's Music and Organizational Culture*, Stacy Holman Jones

Volume 4, *Fiction and Social Research: By Fire or Ice*, Anna Banks and Stephen P. Banks, editors

Volume 5, *Reading Auschwitz*, Mary Lagerwey

Volume 6, *Life Online: Researching Real Experience in Virtual Space*, Annette N. Markham

Volume 7, *Writing the New Ethnography*, H. L. Goodall Jr.

Volume 8, *Between Gay and Straight: Understanding Friendship Beyond Sexual Orientation*, Lisa Tillmann-Healy

Volume 9, *Ethnographically Speaking: Autoethnography, Literature, and Aesthetics*, Arthur P. Bochner and Carolyn Ellis, editors

Volume 10, *Karaoke Nights: An Ethnographic Rhapsody*, Rob Drew

Karaoke Nights

An Ethnographic Rhapsody

ROB DREW

ALTAMIRA
PRESS

A Division of Rowman & Littlefield Publishers, Inc.
Walnut Creek • Lanham • New York • Oxford

ALTAMIRA PRESS
A division of Rowman & Littlefield Publishers, Inc.
1630 North Main Street, #367
Walnut Creek, CA 94596
www.altamirapress.com

Rowman & Littlefield Publishers, Inc.
A wholly owned subsidary of The Rowman & Littlefield Publishing Group, Inc.
4501 Forbes Boulevard, Suite 200
Lanham, MD 20706

PO Box 317
Oxford
OX2 9RU, UK

British Library Cataloguing in Publication Information Available

Library of Congress Cataloging-in-Publication Data

Drew, Rob, 1961–
 Karaoke nights : an ethnographic rhapsody / Rob Drew.
  p. cm.
 Includes bibliographical references.
 ISBN 0-7591-0046-2 (alk. paper)—ISBN 0-7591-0047-0 (pbk. : alk. paper)
  1. Karaoke—Social aspects—United States. 2. Bars (Drinking establishments)—Social
aspects—United States. I. Title.

ML3918.K37 D74 2991
306.4'84—dc21   2001022782

Printed in the United States of America

⊗™ The paper used in this publication meets the minimum requirements of American
National Standard for Information Sciences—Permanence of Paper for Printed Library
Materials, ANSI/NISO Z39.48-1992.

CONTENTS

ACKNOWLEDGMENTS

I'd like to thank the karaoke performers and jockeys who have generously provided me with information, insights, and the pleasure of their performances. I am especially indebted to Kathy Balcom, Keith Blaker, Ray Golley, Sue Golley, Kelly Gorman, Masa Iino, Terry Jones, Dave Kidd, Linda Kidd, Connie Morilak, Chuck Nice, Ken Peterson, Johnny Petillo, Scott Reynolds, Henry Ruiz, Tom Seger, Kenichiro Shimokawa, Karl Siwek, Jeffrey Smith, and Alan Zukof. I also owe thanks to members of the *Jolt* Web site's on-line karaoke forum, the best single source of information on the subject in the United States, where I've been an occasional contributor and constant lurker. *Jolt*'s archives include discussions of every conceivable dimension of karaoke and an inexhaustible fund of ideas and opinions.

The following people have read parts of this book at various stages and offered advice and encouragement: Janaki Bakhle, Elizabeth Bell, Spencer Cahill, Johan Fornäs, Bud Goodall, Andrew Goodwin, Bob Hornik, Henry Jenkins, Doni Loseke, Casey Lum, Toru Mitsui, John Pauly, Janice Radway, Gil Rodman, Greg Seigworth, Lynn Spigel, Bryan Taylor, Joe Turow, Deborah Wong, Charles Wright, and Barbie Zelizer. Four individuals' contributions stand out. Carolyn Marvin has been an advisor and a scholarly model to me, meticulous in her research and totally committed to her students. Larry Gross's insistence on the relevance of artful communication to everyday life, as well as his intellectual breadth and generosity, have deeply influenced my work. Art Bochner and Carolyn Ellis have been editors, cheerleaders, and friends who've vastly enlarged my understanding of what academic research and writing can be.

My colleagues in the Department of Communication at Saginaw Valley State University and former colleagues at the University of South

ACKNOWLEDGMENTS

Florida have supported my work on this book unfailingly and patiently abided my promises that I would contribute more to departmental business once it was done. Many dear friends have helped me make my way through karaoke and much else. They are Pär Bendz, Bill Carney, Dan Finnigan, Dave Finzel, Chris Green, Pam Inglesby, Helen Isenberg, Tom Isenberg, Janna Jones, Charlene Melcher, Mike Mosher, Lexa Murphy, Mark Neumann, Stuart Sigman, Darren Staloff, Susan Stone, and many others. My wife, Amy, my sons, Charlie and Danny, and my brothers, Larry and Ken, have provided love, support, and encouragement every step of the way.

This book is dedicated to my father, who once told me that you could take a good picture of anything if you find the right angle, and my mother, who once told me that when you make a party you should be sure you have enough food.

PROLOGUE
GIVE IT A SHOT

Let me tell you about the time I almost got on a network TV pilot. It's December 1990. I have this harebrained idea about doing my doctoral dissertation on karaoke, the Japanese performance craze that's just begun to infiltrate the United States, but I don't know how to go about it. All I know is that my handful of visits to karaoke bars have yielded some of the most exhilarating experiences of public communication I can remember. "Start where you are," John and Lyn Lofland advise in their book on qualitative research.[1] This is where I am.

Though I live in Philadelphia, I initially travel to New York for my karaoke outings for several reasons. First, I'm not sure I'm ready to sing publicly in the town where I live or anywhere near it. Second, New York is home to the only karaoke bar I know of at the moment. (As it happens, it will be easy to find karaoke bars in Philadelphia. When I begin my research in earnest eight months later, I'll locate forty-five of them in short order.) Third, there's the bar itself, the Vocal Heroes Club in the Hell's Kitchen area of Manhattan. Karaoke performers, no less than rock stars or opera divas, have their favorite locales. Performers who travel far and wide in search of new karaoke scenes still speak lovingly of their "home bars." From the night I first attended Vocal Heroes and, emboldened by whiskey and cigarettes, warbled Harold Melvin and the Blue Notes' "If You Don't Know Me By Now" to a scattered crowd of last-call diehards, there's been something special about the place for me. I look forward to the habitués: the guy who tosses stage money to the crowd as he sings the line "Now Macheath spends like a sailor!" from "Mack the Knife," the Australian who does "My Way" in the voice of Sid Vicious, the young sweethearts who dry-hump their way through "Paradise by the Dashboard Light."

1

So much of social life is anchored by simple devices. A flag is a piece of cloth on a stick. Wafer and wine become body and blood in church. A karaoke system consists of a microphone, a sound system with voice mixer, a video monitor for lyrics, and some recordings of pop songs with the vocals missing. Everything else depends on the people.

And so, my last incentive to go to New York this Saturday night is a person, my friend Bill Carney. In choosing a karaoke companion, you want someone who's seen you at your best and worst, who's heard such noises emanate from you that nothing would surprise him. For me, Bill is that person—besides which, he's the only person I know who's game.

Brothers in arms for years, Bill and I have always maintained fairly polite and diffident public faces and barely concealed a desperate longing to be heard. Now and then, empowered by one another's audience, we've given voice to that longing. In 1982, at the auditions for our college talent show, we ambushed the producers with our purportedly humorous skits. My contribution was loosely based on Plato's *Symposium*, Bill's on the Sex Pistols' "Bodies" (we got thrown out on our asses). In 1985, we drove coast to coast and cold-called the LA office of gonzo record producer Kim Fowley. We fully expected he'd make us stars, despite our having no obvious musical talents and nothing to show but our glorious selves (we got thrown out on our asses). And in May of 1990, it was Bill who phoned me from a hotel bar in Little Rock and told me how some Japanese men in suits were test-marketing some sort of singing machine, and how he'd just sung Lesley Gore's "It's My Party" to a bunch of rednecks who weren't quite sure what to make of him.

But Bill is no Lesley Gore, and I'm no Harold Melvin. In karaoke, as in love, the first time is rarely the most gratifying. You have to be persistent, experiment with different positions, find your comfort zone. Bill and I are two middle-class, white guys in our late twenties. We both grew up in music capitals of sorts, though of very different sorts. Bill is from Detroit, heart of rock and soul; I'm from the Borscht Belt, the Jewish resort area of upstate New York where premodern pop stars like Eddie Fisher and Danny Kaye launched their careers. As of this December evening, Bill has settled into a repertoire of slick country tunes that harmonize his Midwestern roots and his Manhattan coming of age: Merle Haggard's "Mama Tried," Tennessee Ernie Ford's "Sixteen Tons," Dave Dudley's "Six Days on the Road." I myself, for whatever reason, have been seeking solace among the blue-eyed, Reagan-era sounds that I was born too soon and too skeptical to much enjoy—hits from people like Bryan Adams, Foreigner, Bon Jovi, Michael Jackson, and Debbie Gibson.

We sit in Bill's Chelsea apartment and pore over the copy of Vocal Heroes' seven-hundred-song "menu" that I've brought with me. (The selection at some bars will increase fortyfold in the next ten years. Enter a karaoke bar for the first time, get hold of one of these booklets, and you're likely to go through a quick series of impressions. First, you'll think what a joke this is, then you'll marvel at the variety of musical choices, and then you'll come across a song or two that is so *you* that you can hardly keep yourself from volunteering.) Bill gets up and cues up a tune on his tape deck: Bobby Bare's "Detroit City," 23-B-8 on the Vocal Heroes' menu. He steps back and starts singing:

> *Last night I went to sleep in Detroit City*
> *And I dreamed about those cottonfields back home*

It's clear to me that he's practiced alone, though he'd never admit it—no sooner than we'd admit to the people at Vocal Heroes that we'd practiced together. We feel obliged to pretend that there's something fundamentally offhanded and unserious about it all. Bill delivers the lines broadly and smiles now and then.

> *Home folks think I'm big in Detroit City*
> *From the letters that I write they think I'm fine*
> *But by day I make the cars, by night I make the bars*
> *If only they could read between the lines*

For a second, Bill's smile disappears, and I start reading between the lines. Bare's Detroit homelessness seemingly gives voice to Bill's Detroit homesickness. Bare's tale of northern migration and industrial anomie is now Bill's story. Having migrated east from an ailing industrial region, he toils miserably at a corporate law job that seems meaningless compared to his dad's auto plant work. Bare's working-class exploitation provides a metaphor for Bill's stint as overworked yuppie.

> *I wanna go home, I wanna go home,*
> *Oh, how I waaanna go home.*

It's a short walk from Bill's apartment to the club. We flash our ID's and pay our five dollars. Vocal Heroes is one of the few bars to charge even this small cover for karaoke. But then Vocal Heroes is unusual in larger ways, since it's devoted exclusively to karaoke. Most karaoke in the United States is a makeshift affair; emcees[2] are hired for one or two nights a week and must scare up performances in settings that may lack even the basic necessities of a stage and a sound system. Only in New York do whole establishments materialize in response to every latest thing: roller discos, beach clubs, juice bars, and seven-night-a-week karaoke bars.

In most respects, Vocal Heroes resembles any other small music venue. People mill around a large, open space, with the physical bar tucked off to one side. A three-foot-high stage runs the length of the back wall. Rectangular tables with "reserved" signs project out from the stage, mimicking the privileged territory set aside for industry insiders in "real" music clubs. Yet there are signs that you're someplace different. In a loft above the bar sits a technician who works a laser disc player instead of a soundboard. Onstage, instead of a band, there are one or more people singing into microphones, alternately looking out at the crowd and into a small video monitor on a stand that displays the song lyrics in sync with the music. To the side of the singers, a wide-screen monitor faces outward for the audience's benefit.

The performers onstage are likely to appear altogether ordinary—and thus, as onstage performers go, extraordinary. They might be balding or short or overweight or homely. Their clothes might be drab or too tight or too loose. They might hold the mikes awkwardly, and their movements might be vague and wary. They might have trouble stopping themselves from laughing, or they might seem to force a laugh to ease the tension. Often, aside from mouthing the words softly, they may not do very much at all and may seem to be waiting along with the audience for something to happen. And if you're used to seeing performers onstage or on television who are gorgeous, vivacious, and mellifluous, you might very well walk out then and there.

If you hang around long enough, though, something will happen. It might only happen for one performance, or for a brief moment within a performance. Someone will get up on the stage, maybe for the first time, with no expectations and no agenda. She might start off unexceptionally, haltingly. At some point she'll hit a tough note, or render a poignant lyric with the right twist. The crowd will cheer, and she'll take their cue to push further. Suddenly she'll possess the song, and be possessed by it, and surprise everyone, including herself. I've seen it happen to others. On this particular evening, it's my turn.

It seems important not to submit our song choices too hastily, not to seem anxious or overprepared, spontaneity being a fragile condition that must be cultivated or, at times, fabricated. And so we lean on the bar, casually flipping through the song menus and monitoring the action onstage. Eventually, we scribble our names and song choices on the slips of paper provided and bring them up to the host who takes them with a curt nod.

I've taken a risk, choosing a song I've never done before and don't even know very well, number 12-B-10, Bon Jovi's "Livin' on a Prayer." It's about a guy who gets thrown out of work by a strike and has to live off his girlfriend and pawn his guitar—one of those touching, 1980s' tributes to the dignity of the common folk that provided a soundtrack for the real-life trampling of the common folk. It's all so ridiculous. Here I am, the grad student, the intellectual, publicly performing a song more suited to high school girls from Staten Island with big hair and spandex leggings. But there's something in there for me.

We wait, and watch from the bar. We watch a group of clean-cut, fraternity types, introduced by the emcee as "leaving soon for the Middle East," lead the crowd in a rousing version of the national anthem, followed by a collective shout of "Fuck Iraq!" We watch a black man in a leather jacket and t-shirt sing an over-the-top, femme version of Shirley Bassey's "Goldfinger" (*His heart is cold . . . as a witch's tit in a brass bra!*). We watch many other highlights and lowlights until the emcee announces, "Let's all welcome Hank!" and Bill, recognizing his nom de guerre, ascends the stage and launches into "Detroit City."

The cowboys in the crowd recognize the opening chords and shout their approval, and Bill flashes a grin. As he sings, people turn to check him out, this dude with the high voice mouthing his weird, old-time tune. Bill glances at me here and there and I give him the thumbs up. It's different from singing at home—the crowd complicates his performance. He seems to display his effect on the audience partly for my benefit; at the same time, he and I perform our relationship for the sake of the crowd. Yet while managing this subtle interplay, Bill preserves the slight detachment that I've rarely ever seen him breach. He titillates us with glimpses of himself, but ultimately he seems somewhere else, observing the scene from afar.

Oh, how I waaanna go home. As the music fades and the applause mounts, Bill descends from the stage and returns to the bar.

"Nice job," I say, holding out my hand.

He slaps it and says, "Thanks." His voice shakes, and I can see that he is brimming with feeling, and I wonder how he manages never to overflow.

I'm next. I stamp out my fourth cigarette and toss back the last of my third beer. Doing karaoke, it becomes easy to understand how so many pop stars destroy themselves. The truth is that no substance-induced buzz can assure the oscillating state of unselfconsciousness and hyperconsciousness that is the stage performer's bliss. It requires an act of will.

Though I know it is coming, as always, it jars me to hear my name announced. I walk up slowly and experience that weird parallax effect. One moment you're immersed in a crowd; the next, they're oriented, as one, toward you. They're attentive, expectant, making you out. Do something. I sing.

> *Tommy used to work on the docks*
> *Union's been on strike, he's down on his luck*
> *It's tough . . . so tough*

Good, it's in my key. In karaoke, it's always a crapshoot. No rehearsal, no screening, no guarantee that you won't be standing up there for three minutes mutilating your vocal chords, embarrassing yourself and everyone else.

> *Gina works the diner all day*
> *Working for her man, she brings home the pay*
> *For love . . . for love*

Many in the audience sing along with spirit. They know their Bon Jovi, as can be expected from the club's bridge-and-tunnel crowd. That means if I botch it, I'll be twice as culpable—I'll have sullied a canonical text. But if I do okay, I'll have earned their respect. It's a test of sorts, like taking your horn into Minton's in Harlem circa 1942 and blowing "Salt Peanuts."[3]

> *She says, we've gotta hold on to what we've got*
> *Cause it doesn't make a difference if we make it or not*

We've got each other, and that's a lot
For love, we'll give it a shot

The song starts to open up for me. Singing Gina's words for these listeners, the song's "we" is redefined, and redefines us. It's no longer about merely surviving, eking out a living; it's about the performance itself, what we're experiencing here and now—"what we've got." It's about "giving it a shot," taking a risk, allowing yourself to become part of something larger than yourself—and, if you're lucky, transporting and transforming yourself and others. I close my eyes. Here comes the chorus.

Ohh, we're halfway there
Ohh-oh! livin' on a prayer!
You take my hand and we'll make it, I swear
Ohh-oh! livin' on a prayer!

The words boom from the crowd. I wail into the mike, struggling not to be drowned out, rejoicing over what I'm wreaking. This is what I've waited for, the promise I knew karaoke held. To have a voice and be heard. To delight myself and thereby delight others. To make a song my own and dispense it as a gift. The song unfolds like a secret I'm revealing.

Tommy's got his six-string in hock
Now he's holdin' in what he used to make it talk
It's tough . . . so tough

It must be tough. To be denied your instrument of public speech, your power to do what I'm doing now. For those who long to speak but are too busy subsisting, for those who can't imagine the terrific euphoria of speech, for those who are simply afraid.

Gina dreams of runnin' away
When she cries in the night, Tommy whispers
"Baby, it's okay . . . someday"

I, too, whisper, "It's okay," and the crowd seems to sigh, buoyed by my conviction.

. . . Let's give it a shot!

The last chorus kicks in. I'm raving like a lunatic, breathlessly scaling the ohh-oh's, singing through every pore. How long have I been up here? How much longer do I have? Just as I'm hoping it will never end . . . it does.

"Let's have a hand for Rob!" The emcee affords me this generic, closing salute. I descend from the stage, sated and spent. The crowd cheers, and I indulge myself with the feeling that their response to me is above average. But who knows? I want to ask them, Was it as good for you as it was for me?

As I walk back through the crowd, people greet me. "Nice job!" "Bon Jovi!" But the exchanges are strangely attenuated. It's all polite smiles and sidelong glances. None of us are quite sure where I stand.

I return to Bill at the bar. After either of us performs, the other gives him a long look. Maybe I'm waiting for him to explain why he's so cool; maybe he's waiting for me to explain why I'm so crazy. But no explanation is ever forthcoming. We never really will know each other. The mystery is part of what sustains us.

I order another beer, expecting more accolades from the bartender. Instead, he silently serves up my drink, gruff and nonchalant. He sees this every night, I realize. This is how rock stars must feel when dealing with roadies. No one's a hero to his valet.

We're considering putting in for another round onstage, when an artsy-looking guy in black jeans and a turtleneck approaches us and introduces himself. He's producing a pilot for a television network, one of those real-life programs, about the wild and wacky ways people spend their Saturday nights. He's videotaped both our songs and wants permission to use them in his show. Hey, no problem. We sign the release forms, doing our best to act natural.

We decide to call it a night. There's no feeling like leaving the room having impressed everyone present (or believing you have)—even, perhaps especially, when you'll never see them again. Unlike singing pros, karaoke performers can always quit while they're ahead (though they often don't know how to), and tonight Bill and I are way ahead. "Who were those masked men?" I imagine people asking.

On our way home, we laugh openly, deliriously. Our big break! We've been discovered! It's such a joke, yet all our joking can't dilute our sincere joy. Karaoke performers often dream of an audience beyond their bars.

(Months later, as I sit watching performances and taking notes for this study, more than one singer will approach me and ask if I'm a talent scout.) If this is the ultimate goal of karaoke, then we've attained it.

Later, lying in the dark on Bill's foldout couch, I'm sobered by doubts. First, a sense of irony, and then uneasiness, that I, an academic observer, have posed as native for another, a filmic observer. Shouldn't we have declined and directed the guy to some more experienced performers—some more authentic natives?

But what really troubles me is that I evidently care so much about this. I'm supposed to be scouting for a research topic. Instead, I'm running around bars making a fool of myself, elated when a TV camera happens to catch my charade. What do I expect to come of this? Who do I think I'm kidding?

Wired on cigarettes, I lie half awake for hours, the words of the song I performed reeling through my head like an oppressive mantra. The next morning, I have a breakfast date with an old girlfriend I haven't seen in years. Hungover and drawn, I put in another performance, this one dismal.

Two months pass and I call the TV producer. He's finished the pilot but the network has passed on it. I study the media for a living, so I'm fully aware that most pilots produced for television are never aired. I'm still disappointed.

The producer kindly sends me a copy of the pilot, my first recording of myself as karaoke performer. (Such recordings are common possessions among experienced performers; karaoke is nothing if not reflexive. Many emcees will sell you a video of your performance for a small price, and some give away cheap audiocassettes for free.)

I stick the tape in my VCR and fast-forward to the karaoke segment. A montage of performers parades across the screen. I find myself watching them, not through the eyes of a crowd member in a karaoke bar, but through those of a television viewer—a role to which I am more accustomed. Before long, it is clear to me that this program would not have made a celebrity of anyone. In the world of television, there seem to be two types of people: those who belong there and those who don't. The markers that lent character to performers onstage render them hopelessly out of place on television. Not having received the television treatment of makeup and wardrobe, the performers don't look very different from the petty offenders rounded up every day on *Cops*. If real life is what you want, then real life is what you get.

Whereas the karaoke bar experience can be totally absorbing, its televised version induces couch-potato cynicism. I watch as two overweight, middle-aged guys—one with nerdy glasses, the other with his shirt collar folded unfashionably over his sweater—do a monotone rendition of "You've Lost That Lovin' Feelin'." Five college girls squeal "Like A Virgin" as their excessive makeup starts to run under the hot lights. Two boys in acid-washed jeans, dress shirts, and gold chains (from Long Island, no doubt) stand stiffly, lumbering through a Buttafuoco-esque version of "Brandy."

Then there's Bill. Just the sight of the guy is enough to lift me. But watching him with his chin in the air and his eyes half open, pumping his arms slightly, and tossing the mike from one hand to the other (his signature move), even Bill, who seemed so understated and cool at the bar, now seems kind of dull.

And then there's me. I'm struck by how fat I look—not yet late-Elvis fat, but still fat. I'm struck by how drab my clothes look, how messy my hair looks, how puffy my face looks, how profusely I sweat, how clumsily I move, how flatly I sing. More than anything, I'm struck by the disparity between everything I see on that screen, and everything I felt on that stage.

And I know one thing. I'll believe what I feel over what I see any day.

CHAPTER ONE
KARAOKE STATESIDE

First, a word on what this book isn't about. It's not about karaoke's history, its beginnings in the seaport towns of Japan, its swift incursion into the after-hours regimen of Japan's business class, its diffusion throughout East Asia and, eventually, to most every human outpost on the planet. It's not about the technology of karaoke, early analog systems, later digital systems, systems with key changers and echo effects and choral effects, the system developed at MIT's Media Lab that adjusts a song's tempo to your singing, or the one devised by an Oxford linguist that morphs your voice into Elvis's or Maria Callas's. It's not about nursery school karaoke, or nursing home karaoke, or Christian karaoke, or nudist karaoke. Not about the "punk karaoke" concert tour of 1998, where audience members were invited to caterwaul through their favorite hardcore tunes backed by a crack band of punk scene veterans. Not about the fabulous London and New York runs of "The Karaoke Sound of Music," where mostly gay audiences clad in lederhosen and nun's habits and Nazi regalia played the chorus for a subtitled, bouncing-ball version of the saccharine movie musical. Not about the New York businessman who airlifted a karaoke system to a refugee camp in Albania during the Kosovo crisis. The point, not to belabor it, is that there are many karaokes, and there are likely to be many more.[1]

This book, though, is about karaoke in bars. For in spite of every effort by retailers to market it for home use, karaoke continues to fare best in public—above all, in these most mundane and accessible of public contexts. It's impossible to guess how many karaoke bars there are in the United States; karaoke is too dispersed and dynamic, too much the movable feast, to allow for any such reckoning. The most credible survey I've come across was launched by the moderators of the *Jolt* Web site's on-line karaoke forum, which in May of 1998 issued a call for contributors to post their favorite places to sing. Within a year, they'd received word of more than 1,500 bars in 50 states.[2] Based as it is on a volunteer sampling of karaoke enthusiasts who happen to be Internet denizens, the *Jolt* survey doubtless only scratches the surface. Some of these bars host karaoke only one night a week, others have it two, three, or seven nights. Some run their own shows using their own equipment, others hire independent emcees or regional outfits with stables of emcees. Some draw tiny crowds of regulars, others can attract dozens of performers and hundreds of onlookers. Practically all karaoke bars, though, offer an onstage turn to anyone, regardless of vocal ability or criminal history or legal sanity, for nothing more than the variable costs of liquid courage.

Yet comparatively few of us in the United States have taken up karaoke on even a casual basis. For all our democratic ideals, we're famously unschooled in the art of public communication, in getting up and expressing ourselves before an audience. Add to this our conditioned fear of singing, as well as our reluctance to go public with the often personal, emotional content of popular music, and karaoke's challenge can seem Herculean. No wonder that the very mention of the thing so often provokes nervous laughter; our knee-jerk response is to make a joke of it. This book attempts to take karaoke's promise seriously and put it to the test. Through ethnographic study, I'll consider how this seemingly exotic variety of vocal performance has become, for many, an everyday ritual, taking on deep personal and social significance in the process. This is an up-close and personal account of how karaoke is achieved, and what is achieved by it.

The Cosmic and the Local

The idea that public singing could be a weekly or nightly routine, as banal as beer and as casual as conversation, is hard for Americans to get used to. We're baffled to learn that more than half of all Japanese perform karaoke in a year, or that 80 percent of Japan's 350,000 bars are equipped with karaoke systems.[3] But then, throughout much of Asia, singing has long been de rigueur at all sorts of gatherings, an essential catalyst to social and professional relationships. A friend of mine who taught in Hong Kong for a year once got the notion to invite her grad students over for the sort of end-of-the-semester confab that young American professors fancy. When she suggested it to one student, he thought for a minute and asked her if she had a karaoke machine. She replied that she didn't. He asked if she was planning on getting one, and she said that she wasn't. The student looked down. "Well," he said coyly, "What *are* we going to do?"

In comparison, Americans rarely come up against circumstances where they're expected or particularly encouraged to sing. Though we're surrounded by music nearly everywhere, many of us see musical creation not as an everyday form of communication but as an occult affair marked off by concert stages and studio walls. It's become a platitude of cultural history that Americans don't make music anymore—that, over the past century and a half, amateur and regional forms of music and leisure have been superceded by mediated, commercial forms.[4] The case is easily overstated. Plenty of music is being made out there, much of it aided by the very technologies that are commonly blamed for killing music making.[5] The parlor piano has given way to the Casio keyboard, hip-hop and dance musicians have turned cutting and mixing into an artful mode of performance, and pretty much every town has its complement of rock and pop bands that slog it out on the local bar circuit. Yet much of this musical activity is hidden from view, its media presence confined to occasional radio interviews and write-ups at the back of free weeklies. And when it does get noticed, local music is often reduced to a mere auxiliary of the national music system, a limbolike state in the quest for tours, record contracts, and chart success. In the eyes of the press, the profiteers, the public, and many of the musicians themselves, local music stands as something to get *beyond*.[6]

The reduction of local music to an appendage of the national makes its way into karaoke circles as well. Whereas in Japan, karaoke is seen as many things—a skill, an etiquette, a cultural emblem, a health aid, a purification rite, an aphrodisiac[7]—in the United States, it is seen overwhelmingly as one thing: a chance to "be a star." The promise of stardom is ballyhooed constantly in press accounts of karaoke, in ads for karaoke bars and services, and in emcees' onstage patter. The precise meaning of the karaoke-as-stardom equation is often unclear, in part because the meaning of stardom itself is so elusive. Sometimes it seems only to refer to the outer trappings of stardom; the background music, the guaranteed applause, the microphones and spotlights are said to substantiate fantasies we've harbored since childhood when we hopped around our bedrooms and crooned into curling irons. Other times, karaoke stardom translates as a kind of local celebrity. Indeed, a certain buzz often follows the most charismatic singers on the local karaoke circuit whose performances might be greeted with a flourish of cigarette lighters or a hail of apartment keys. Still other times, a more literal stardom is hinted at. Nationwide contests sponsored by karaoke manufacturers reward winners with single releases and TV appearances, while shadier outfits organize "showcases" at local clubs and offer vanity-label record contracts to *any* reasonably talented singer—for a price. And still other times, metaphors of stardom applied to karaoke seem only to constitute a vague code for being the center of attention, for being granted a momentary public voice.

This force-fitting of karaoke and of all local music within the logic of stardom says much about stardom's spell over contemporary American culture. In the early twentieth century, pop stars (like film stars) served mainly to stabilize demand for cultural products and put a human face on the new mass media. The supply of stars was restricted, and stars were trumpeted as miraculously gifted individuals, as in the fan magazine cults of pop stars from Bing Crosby to the Beatles. Yet, since around the time Andy Warhol's "famous for fifteen minutes" forecast became a household phrase, the material and ideological foundations of celebrity have shifted. The manufacture of celebrities has become more controlled yet more free ranging, higher in output but also in turnover. Legions of gossip reporters and publicity flacks scour every corner of society seeking new candidates for the mantle of celebrity, selling the prospect of stardom at one end while selling stars at the other.[8] In the music industry, giant entertainment firms reach from corporate centers to the farthest margins of local music. Becoming a pop star nowadays is less like climbing a ladder and more like being shot out of a cannon. Musicians and entire music scenes are thrust into the orbit of superstardom in wheel-of-fortune fashion, like overvalued stocks.[9]

Yet even as the production of celebrity becomes ever more transparent and routine, its pursuit seems ever more urgent and its grip on our imagination of public life ever more secure. Celebrities have always enacted "a spectacle of individuality,"[10] a play of power and freedom on behalf of the majority of us slaving away at our humble callings. Nowadays, though, stars arouse discontentment and envy as much as identification.

Stardom looms like a random state of grace meted out from above, so that those of us unblessed with it "run the danger of being, in our own eyes, unpersons."[11] At the same time, the language of celebrity gnaws its way under the skin of our most familiar rituals; stardom becomes a trope for any sort of public life or public agency. "You're the star today," we say to the graduate in procession, the newlyweds, the Bar Mitzvah boy (the events themselves seem modeled on Hollywood conventions). Surveying the rust belt of northern England with its pockets of protected wilderness, Geoff Dyer writes, "These days we scarcely even notice ugliness. We notice its absence."[12] That's how it is with stardom. These days we scarcely notice our anonymity, our smallness of voice. We notice its absence, which we call stardom.

I don't wish to trivialize karaoke's rhetoric of stardom or the conditions and desires that shape it. A critique of this rhetoric too easily dovetails with depictions of karaokists as wannabes who cultivate over-rich fantasy lives ("a strange subculture of regulars who meet at the same places every week to act out their Big Time Pop Star fantasies for each other," reads one eloquent cynic's description).[13] Karaoke performers are no more wannabes than any other local musicians, and often no less capable. A few performers have, in fact, enjoyed national success. Country darling Mindy McCready is said to have parlayed her karaoke tapes into a major label contract, teen singer Lina Santiago went from karaoke contests at Los Angeles restaurants to a national Top 10 dance hit, Canadian stage star Tyler Ross got his break when a casting agent spotted him singing karaoke at a party.[14] Many more performers have drawn on karaoke for the confidence and the kick-in-the-butt to join local bands or church choirs or theater troupes, or simply to sing (or speak) publicly in other contexts for the first time. As karaoke has taken root in the United States, its ties with local music scenes have strengthened. Bands sometimes use karaoke to scout out and audition vocal talent, while professional singers turn to karaoke to keep their voices supple and their egos intact between gigs.[15]

A karaoke bar may, then, be as good a starting point as any for an aspiring superstar. All music is ultimately local in origin. Among the tangled tributaries of the world's music, the local feeds and is fed by the national and international constantly. Yet it needs to be understood that local music has an integrity of its own—that much of the pleasure and danger of local music stems from precisely those qualities that distinguish it from national music. More than anything, what draws people to local music scenes is the promise of a music that touches their daily lives and relationships. In studies of music scenes such as those by Ruth Finnegan, Sara Cohen, and Barry Shank, we find individuals whose musical affiliations—as fellow performers, as performers and listeners—are intricately interwoven with their personal affiliations.[16] Often, the members of local musical groups are schoolmates or workmates or childhood playmates who've hammered away at instruments together in each other's basements for years. Often, they play for small, intimate audiences composed largely of friends and relatives. Where stars are cloistered within the unreal spaces of recording studios and arena stages, local musicians make their appearances along the well-trodden pathways of communities, in bars and clubs, schools and churches, fairs and festivals. Where stars are known for their intermittent recordings and tours, local musicians often hew to a monthly or weekly schedule that becomes as habitual for audiences as it is for performers.

As a form of local music, karaoke, too, is steeped in everyday, collective life. Almost always, people make their first forays into karaoke bars and onto karaoke stages, flanked by friends or lovers or coworkers. As people warm to the lifestyle and acquaint themselves with the local karaoke circuit, new cliques are formed, singing partners swapped, social and musical combinations tested. Ask any performer why she chose a certain song or rendered it a certain way, and she's likely to cite social factors: a sense of the crowd's mood, an inside joke with a friend, a romance or the inkling of one. Performers preface their songs with dedications and sprinkle them with acknowledgments of companions on- and offstage. They wink and whisper, throw their friends kisses, or give them the finger. "I believe if there is a God, he doesn't exist in any one of us, but in the little space between us," says a character in Richard Linklater's movie *Before Sunrise*. Music, too, finds its life between us, nowhere more so than in karaoke.

Yet the social synergy of local music practices like karaoke shouldn't be sentimentalized or overstated. These are not Boy Scouts chanting "Kumbaya" around the campfire; there is a darker side to local music scenes as well. There are the ego trips and strained friendships, the musical differences that get personal, and the personal differences that get played out through music. Most of all, there is the frightening immediacy of local music. The "theatrical frame" of local performance, the set of spatial and temporal markers that insulate it from the social world offstage, is uniquely loose and ambiguous.[17] Cohen hints at this when describing her Liverpool musicians' dread of mingling with audiences after performances—and one band member's preoccupation with his mother's presence in the crowd as his mates drunkenly flail onstage.[18] Local performances such as those undertaken in karaoke bars are, in every sense, close to home—proximate and consequential in ways that star performances can't be. Where stars take refuge in green rooms and limousines, local performers emerge from and return to the crowd. Where stars rove around the country or the world, an audience in every port, locals don't leave. Like the very rich—those whom Paul Fussell calls "top out-of-sights"—stars can stave off, and sometimes feel the need to barricade themselves against, the Sartrean hell of other people.[19] Locals are thoroughly enmeshed within it.

And where stars can finally justify what they do as their livelihood, most local performers are amateurs who make little or no money from their performances. This leaves them, as Robert Stebbins writes, on the margins of modern leisure, "neither dabblers who approach the activity with little commitment or seriousness, nor professionals who make a living from that activity."[20] On one side, the local performer finds the friends and relatives to whom she must explain spending several nights a week on an apparently profitless pursuit. On the other, she finds the professional performers who, though she models herself upon them, seem forever to regard her as a second-class dilettante. Thus karaokists and all local musicians must deal with the sense of redundancy that comes from making local music in a culture dominated by mass music. Like the kids who set off M-80s along the crowd's periphery at Fourth of July celebrations, they're often regarded as a noisy, pesky distraction from the Big Show. The stock put-down of local performers, as of all who take their leisure too seriously, is "get a life"—a life, for too many of us, boiling down to a job, a family, a pair of slippers and a TV set.[21]

All of this makes local music an accomplishment—and begs the question of how it is accomplished. Karaoke performers, no less than other local performers, routinely put themselves on the line in ways stars don't have to. Despite their paucity of formal training, they take the stage under conditions so unstructured and unpredictable, that many trained singers would be frightened off. They risk failure in the most intimate, diffuse performance contexts, where failure can feel very personal. Performers willingly shoulder this burden on behalf of the radical notion that culture is ordinary—that music is not marginal to daily life, something to be supplied by a chosen few artists, but a necessary part of living.[22] In karaoke, we find people devising ways to break the silence of a nonperforming, nonsinging culture; maybe we get an idea how we can do so ourselves.

Puttin' on the Hits

In 1992, when the media blitz surrounding its stateside arrival peaked, karaoke won the dubious distinction of a citation in a presidential campaign speech, as George Bush found a way to use it against the ascendant Clinton-Gore ticket. "Don't kid yourselves, America," Bush told a crowd in Houston, "We're not running against the comeback kids. We're running against the karaoke kids, and they'll sing any tune they think will get them elected."[23] The implication was that the Democrats were frauds—and, incidentally, that karaoke was a fraudulent art. Yet Bush failed to acknowledge his own rhetorical debts. Only a few months earlier, a member of British Prime Minister John Major's cabinet had tagged the Labour Party leader Neil Kinnock in almost identical terms, "Karaoke Kinnock . . . he'll sing any song you want him to."[24] Indeed, reading their prepared material from TelePrompTers, how many of our postmodern political orators could stand to reflect upon the origins of their own tunes?

Among possible descriptors for karaoke, "original" is not one that springs to mind. "If music is supposed to be a sound-producing endeavor expressing individual thoughts and feelings with the creativity and spontaneity of the moment," writes Christine Yano, "then karaoke does not exactly fit the mold."[25] Karaoke involves what Erving Goffman famously called a "keying," a transformation of a preexisting activity into something patterned upon yet different from itself.[26] And a karaoke performance is a complex, multilayered sort of keying, for its template is not a written set of lyrics, nor even a song composition, but a full-blown, prior performance—a popular recording. Like professional cover versions of pop songs (only more so), a karaoke number "iterates . . . a prior recorded performance of a song by a particular artist, rather than simply the song itself as an entity separate from any performer or performance."[27] The best karaoke software manufacturers, the ones whose discs are prized most by performers, are those who make an effort to replicate every sonic minutia of the original hits, those whose video-fed lyric displays include the most offhanded phrasings of the original vocalists. Karaoke, then, is the most scripted sort of song performance imaginable. Its communicative possibilities are both opened up and closed off by its layered context of lyrics, background music, and prior performance. And its reception in different cultural contexts reflects differing attitudes toward the potential and power of so scripted a vocal performance.

If one thing strikes Western observers of Eastern karaoke, it is its imitativeness. Yano, for instance, observes how Japanese karaoke singers "listen repeatedly to the hit songs as sung by professional singers, attempting to emulate every inflection, ornament, and nuance."[28] Such a mode of performance can easily play into Western stereotypes of Japanese conformity, and so needs to be understood against the backdrop of Japanese culture. In Japan, imitation is understood as a necessary phase in the acquisition of many valued cultural skills.[29] Traditional Japanese arts such as martial arts, calligraphy, and flower arrangement are distinguished by the suffix *dô*, or "way" (*budô, shodô, kadô*). Authorized masters preside over each art and pass them down by modeling stylized series of actions. The martial arts student begins with "mechanical copying of what he sees, repeated to the point of repletion"; the archery student must do no more at first than "conscientiously copy what the teacher shows him."[30] Such imitation eventually becomes the basis for subtle (often invisible, to Western eyes) expressions of creativity and individuality. Yet it is not thought possible to learn an art and use it creatively without first imitating it; the inexplicable, somatic "way" of the art can only be internalized through doing. Michael Polanyi's comments on the importance of "learning by example" to cultural continuity are a tribute to this traditional Japanese attitude:

> To learn by example is to submit to authority. You follow your master because you trust his manner of doing things even when you cannot analyze and account in detail for its effectiveness. By watching the master and emulating his efforts in the presence of his example, the apprentice unconsciously picks up the rules of the art, including those which are not explicitly known to the master himself. These hidden rules can be assimilated only by a person who surrenders himself to that extent uncritically to the imitation of another. A society which wants to preserve a fund of personal knowledge must submit to tradition.[31]

This mode of conduct, rooted in Japan's most austere and esoteric disciplines, courses through the nation's mercurial popular culture. It is only half-jokingly that the Japanese speak of a *karaoke-dô*, a way of karaoke. "Although some might feel that the use of *dô* to refer to something as frivolous as karaoke is inappropriate, this is how some of its practitioners describe the art of singing a song."[32] And it comes as no surprise that in addition to its effects on nightlife, karaoke has sparked a cottage industry in singing instruction in Japan. "How much tuition have you paid?" has become a standard gibe directed at karaoke prodigies.[33]

Yet the real "masters" under whom Japanese karaokists study are not their singing teachers, but the *enka* balladeers and Western-style pop stars of the Japanese recording industry. Indeed, one of the most conspicuous effects of karaoke in Japan has been its invigoration of the country's music business.[34] Starting in the early 1990s, largely due to the introduction of arcade-style karaoke rooms, the craze spread from the late-night, high-priced world of "salarymen" to the general population. This intensified the demand for Japanese-language pop music, as "one of the important elements for hit songs changed from 'good to listen to' to 'good to sing.'"[35] Up until 1990, there had never been more than three regionally produced, million-selling singles in a year; since 1992, there have never been less than thirteen. Japanese record companies now include vocal-less versions on many CD singles for home practice and release song types popular with karaokists (such as duets) in greater numbers. All this suggests a particular way of receiving not only karaoke but popular songs themselves. The song confronts people not as an inviolate object but as a cultural resource; the recording artist stands less as an author or owner, more as a teacher of the song. In Japan, songs are for singing, the tools through which one learns to sing, displays singing competence, adopts singing roles.

By contrast, within the elite cultural tradition of the West, what is most valued in music, as in all art, is the creative output of a singular mind. Great art is regarded as "the product of creative genius that transcends tradition and convention."[36] Communication itself, in the dominant Western model, only takes place when new information is imparted from one mind to another.[37] We've grown accustomed to hearing such arguments deployed against popular culture, which is so often dismissed as homogeneous and unoriginal, yet they're also often floated from *within* popular culture.[38] Among rock musicians and critics, there is no more stinging epithet than "derivative"—this despite the fact that most rockers learn their craft, *dô*-style, by imitating live or mediated mentors. Such an aesthetic tends to undervalue not just formulaic or familiar music, but any sort of musical activity that doesn't involve sitting down and writing songs; witness the Liverpool rockers interviewed by Cohen who regard "the creation and performance of original material" as "integral to a band's self-respect."[39] Hence the low status frequently accorded cover versions. As Simon Frith notes, "One aspect of learning to be a rock fan in the 1960s was . . . learning to prefer originals over covers."[40]

If cover versions are, according to one influential view, bad popular music, then karaoke performances can't be anything more than bad cover versions. As Johan Fornäs writes, "a conservative critic might see karaoke as yet another example of how . . . personal authenticity is removed and replaced by insipid copies of idols."[41] In the Anglo-American lexicon, karaoke often serves as a metaphor for anything deemed shopworn or soulless. A shot-for-shot remake of Hitchcock's *Psycho* is "the film equivalent of karaoke." An Italian designer's Japanese-influenced fashion line is "karaoke couture."[42] And any musician whose live performances parrot her recordings, or who uses recorded material in her live shows, or who simply sounds too much like some other musician evokes instant comparisons to karaoke. Predictably, as it gains a foothold in Euro-American nightlife, the specter arises of karaoke *replacing* live entertainment. Like sound technologies from the microphone to the drum machine, karaoke gets accused of substituting the "direct" encounters of "real" musical performance with a body-snatcher inhumanity. "It's so anti-music," says a former talent booker for a Toronto rock club turned karaoke bar, "so anti-life."[43]

While it's unlikely to snuff out live music any time soon, the larger issue is whether karaoke's derivativeness limits its cultural value. If it must, a case can be made for karaoke's aesthetic worth; much of its artfulness consists precisely in wresting something meaningful from so scripted a context. With chart success and heavy rotation, pop records acquire an aura of inevitability; songs that once were full of surprises quickly get tiresome. Only a skilled karaokist can take a song that seems like a known quantity and put it across in a way that's intense, personal, real—a first, an event. Moreover, though the background music is

21

programmed, the performer needn't be. Anyone who's witnessed a karaokist deliver Helen Reddy's "I Am Woman" in the voice of Arnold Schwarzenegger, or sing the "Gilligan's Island" theme to the tune of "Amazing Grace," or recast John Lennon's love songs as love-of-food songs ("Woman" as "Chicken," "Starting Over" as "Eating Leftovers") might dispute karaoke's lack of originality.

Yet it would be a mistake to judge all karaoke performers against such quirky, clever (and rare) examples. Too often, we evaluate musical performances based on their novelty, their assemblage of new sounds and utterances, or new combinations of melody and lyric and dialect. By this reckoning, musical activities stand or fall on what is written or conceived or "composed." Yet most of us don't compose songs; we embody and enact them. We move to their rhythms, quote snatches of them at odd moments—and sing them. Whether faithful or foolish, visionary or prosaic, a song performance is an exercise in role playing. "All songs are implied narratives," writes Frith. "They have a central character, the singer; a character with an attitude, in a situation, talking to someone (if only to herself)."[44] No less than stage actors, singers don vocal costumes and momentarily succumb to vocal alter egos. Even chiming along with canned accompaniment to an indifferent crowd in a dive at the edge of nowhere, a singer locates herself within the history of her song and the complex of meanings that derive from its genre and lyrics and prior performances.

Through their selections and renderings of songs, then, karaoke performers position themselves psychically, socially, culturally. Accounts of karaoke in Asian American communities affirm its capacity to define and sustain identity. When Vietnamese immigrants sing tangos in suburban Los Angeles karaoke bars, they summon a tortuous musical and cultural history. Tangos, imported from Argentina to Europe and its colonial outposts as far back as the 1930s, then banned by Vietnam's Communist rulers in the 1970s, reappear in karaoke versions among Vietnamese Americans in the 1990s. For these middle- and upper-middle-class émigrés, slaving away at small businesses in the sprawling city of glass, the tango revives a bit of the decadent glamour of a pre-Communist past.[45]

For the youngest generation of Hong Kong immigrants who live in and around New York's Chinatown, Cantonese opera was always "old people's music"; few ever enjoyed it before leaving their homeland. Yet it is these same young immigrants who have formed singing clubs around karaoke versions of Cantonese opera songs. Karaoke here contributes to the fabrication of a tradition among members of a diaspora culture. It evokes dim memories of childhood visits to rural festivals where opera music blended with the sights of games and gamblers and the smells of stewed meats and noodles. The music's themes of piety and chastity form a counterpoint to the liberal, Western-influenced songs popular among most young Chinese Americans. A past is being filled in by these singers, one very different from the immigrant culture they've inherited.[46]

What distinguishes English-language karaoke from its Asian versions is that it is so thoroughly dominated by mass-mediated, popular music. In mainstream U.S. culture, media texts and genres increasingly provide people with their most potent sources of self-definition. "Musical taste is now intimately tied into personal identity; we express ourselves through our deployment of other people's music."[47] The musical menu of a typical American karaoke bar includes thousands of songs in dozens of categories, a pop treasure trove that will fit most any performer with a suitable vocal façade. Performers can express themselves through song and announce their devotion to particular artists and genres, or they can momentarily transcend themselves by singing against type. There is the potential not only for display, but also for fantasy and epiphany. "By trying on Madonna's or Michael Jackson's provocative style of expression, Sinatra's maturity or Sid Vicious' cynical brutality," Fornäs observes, "one might discover new potentials within oneself."[48]

Yet karaoke is not just a personal resource for defining and reinventing selves; it's also a social resource. A karaoke performer positions his audience as well as himself. Consciously or not, he speaks for them and makes a claim on them, offering a particular vision of their realities and possibilities. No less than any other song performance, a karaoke performance carries a normative force and sets a standard for community and contestation. To understand song performance as such challenges us to put aside our fetish for the original and acknowledge the social utility of already-made music. Witness the drag queens who nostalgically conjure a pre-AIDS, gay milieu through lip-synced renditions of old recordings by Shirley Bassey and Tallulah Bankhead; the star impersonators who use Presley and Morrison and Madonna as vehicles to tell stories about their own and their audiences' past and present lives; the cover bands who, even while playing near-rote versions of Top 40 hits at interchangeable hotel lounges, take pride in their ability to please their audiences by reanimating radio music in a live context.[49]

Even on the pop charts, cover records have proliferated recently, "done in every conceivable way . . . ranging from radical modification to slavish imitation."[50] Though it's often framed in the cataclysmic terms of postmodernism, this trend can as easily be understood as a move from the heady creativity of post-sixties popular music to a period of archiving and taking stock. What music do people deem worthy of replaying and remembering? What merits a lasting contribution to cultural and subcultural identity? What music remains powerful and what has become laughable? Such struggles over legacy are played out every day, not just over the airwaves and in the concert arenas, but in miniature every time a karaoke performer uses the stage as a bully pulpit to make a case for the enduring significance of his chosen number.

Ethnography with a Passion

This book explores the issues sketched out so far—issues of popular music and its local performance, of music making and its local accomplishment—through an ethnography of karaoke bars. Ethnography is the research method of observing and participating in human associations in their natural settings. It is also the art of documenting and representing, of understanding and dramatizing such associations. Rather than herding people into a laboratory or canvassing them with a questionnaire, ethnographers meet people where they live and try to do justice to their lives there. Though it's traditionally been the province of anthropologists and sociologists, over the past two decades, experts in communication and cultural studies have turned to ethnography as a way of fathoming the significance of media and commercial culture in modern life. Much of this work has proven valuable for its frontline accounts of how people wrest a sense of identity and agency from the often chaotic, oppressive turnout of the modern mass media. At the same time, this work has come under criticism for its theoretical abstruseness, its superficial fieldwork practices, and its cryptic style of prose.[51]

It's widely agreed that if media ethnography is to continue to grow, it must become more imaginative in its choice of fieldwork contexts and in its conduct of fieldwork. Janice Radway writes that ethnography must move beyond the "habitual practice of conducting bounded, regionalized investigations of singular text-audience circuits."[52] In other words, ethnographers have too often reduced the complex role of media in modern life to observations of people's encounters with particular media texts and genres (or, more commonly, to interviews with people regarding these encounters). Such investigations cannot fully come to terms with either the daunting power or the capacious utility of the media. They tend to both understate people's creativity and overstate people's control in their engagements with the media. Few people nowadays linger within particular "audiences" long enough for researchers to monitor them; indeed, the media are so enmeshed in our lives that the term "audience" no longer describes us adequately.[53] We are (as computer wonks would have it) "users" of the media, actively incorporating bits and pieces of media content into our personal and social lives. But we are also "subjects" of the media, which invade and pervade our lives willy-nilly in all their dizzying hybridity.

I've been drawn to karaoke, in part, as a vehicle to size up the presence of one media form, popular music, in modern life (a form, incidentally, long relegated to the margins of media studies). On the one hand, karaoke bars are places where popular songs are performed and interpreted. On the other hand, they're sites of everyday music making and everyday interaction, where songs form but one thread of the drama, one current in the flow of communication. Songs function as "messages" in karaoke—performers transmit them, audiences receive them—yet from another angle, they act more as context—fading into the background, making meaning around the edges, only thrusting themselves forward now and then on account of some dubious lyric or striking delivery. People use songs in karaoke to define themselves and influence others, yet just as often, songs seem to use people, putting words in their mouths and voices in their heads, some of them apparently meaningless, others terribly meaningful. Songs do things in karaoke bars, they seduce and repulse, embolden and embarrass, connect and divide. Within these humble confines, I hope to catch a sense of how pop music penetrates our selves and relations, how our experience of media "exceeds the time-space of engagement and overflows unpredictably into the process of living."[54]

On its face, karaoke seems a fairly simple object for ethnography, the sort of bounded, exotic practice that makes ideal grist for undergraduate methods classes. Go to a bar, watch some performances, maybe sing yourself if you can find it in you, talk to some people. I did all this on about 140 occasions at 30 different bars, on and off over the course of 6 years (1991–1997), mostly in and around the 3 cities I happened to call home during these years (Philadelphia; Albany, New York; and Tampa, Florida). I located some bars through newspapers and phone books, and many more through subsequent contacts with performers and emcees. I observed thousands of performances, focusing on performers' appearances, song choices, and manner of delivery. I also kept an eye on the action surrounding performances, including crowd response and performers' pre- and post-performance behavior. And I performed many times, alone and with others, focusing here on my own experience of performance and on others' reactions to me.

My understanding of karaoke was aided by the many short- and long-term relationships I formed at the bars, often supplemented by phone conversations and meetings outside the bar context. Some talks were tape-recorded and structured by a short questionnaire dealing with the respondent's prior karaoke experience, details of whatever performances of the respondent's I had observed, and demographic information. Far more talks were spontaneous and informal in tone. I never hid my purpose as a researcher, though in many conversations it never came up. I took prodigious notes, sometimes writing on site, other times on forays to the restroom, or at home from memory. All names in the book (of bars as well as individuals) are pseudonyms, a practice complicated by the fact that many karaoke people are proud of what they do, but settled upon in the august pursuit of legal prophylaxis.

When applied to karaoke, though, this standard ethnographic routine gets complicated. First, how to choose the bars? Karaoke bars are almost too easy to find, yet they're as diverse as bars themselves, and the shape karaoke takes within any venue is affected by everything from layout and décor to the cultural landscape of the community and region. Second, whom to talk to? Who counts as a "native" in karaoke? At many bars, you'll find people who insist on singing, those who sing reluctantly, those who are happy to watch, and those (often holdovers from the bar's pre-karaoke days) who would just as soon see it all go away. There are those who practically live for karaoke, those who show up now and then on a lark, and those who are bribed or forced to attend. In fact, karaoke tends to be particularly popular at places like hotel lounges and resort town clubs—places where most customers pass through rather than settle in, and where they're more likely to happen upon karaoke than seek it out.

Many karaoke bars are, thus, cultural border zones, traversed by regulars and dabblers, tourists and townies, regional and ethnic subgroups. Even steady performers rarely stay put for the ethnographer's gaze. As with other forms of local music, the "circuit" or "scene" is a more relevant unit for many karaokists than any particular venue. Performers move between bars and between scenes, and their onstage and offstage performances often vary with their movements in revealing ways. And bars themselves fall in and out of favor, sometimes scrapping karaoke and pulling the rug out from under any lingering performers and ethnographers. Karaoke thus suffers (or thrives) from the same vexing conditions as so many forms of community in our time: it's diffuse, precarious, crosscut with lasting allegiances and brief encounters.[55]

Studying karaoke ethnographically also poses personal challenges. Ethnographers are often counseled on the perils of "going native" by identifying too closely with those whom they observe. Yet with karaoke, going native is not just a temptation, it's more like an imperative. Karaoke seems to demand participation, and while it's conceivable to study it without performing, my own personal and professional interest in it arose in tandem, so that the task of accounting for others' participation in it has never been separable from the task of accounting for my own. After looking into the eyes of various once-a-year karaokists and telling them that you not only attend karaoke bars several times a week but write about it too, it gets difficult to maintain a clear distinction between observer and observed. And while methodologists may advise that you avoid going native by "keep[ing] in contact with fellow researchers and/or friends with whom these problems can be discussed, placed in context, and weighed," this can get difficult too.[56] A topic like karaoke spills over into your personal life; you become deeply identified with it. Friends and colleagues are eager to share their own karaoke stories and to join you on bar outings. Others with neither experience nor interest in karaoke may know enough from its media representations to tender some question, opinion, or wisecrack. Often you have to fake a laugh when asked if you're bringing your karaoke machine to a department meeting or a job interview or your child's birth. (There is also the issue of karaoke's triviality in many minds, and of the "courtesy stigma" that attaches to researchers on account of their topics, but that's my problem and not yours.)[57] As is bound to happen when studying a topic that hits home—that you and others have intense experiences and strong feelings about—you become a kind of walking field site, and your topic becomes a kind of "total institution" of the mind.

I've done my best to cope with karaoke's multisited messiness and to keep pace with its peripatetic movements. I've gone to every kind of karaoke bar I could locate. In the Philadelphia area alone, I visited white-collar happy-hour bars, downtown dance clubs, college student haunts, suburban neighborhood bars, a sushi bar in Center City, a tourist bar on the Jersey shore, and a redneck bar in rural Pennsylvania. I've attended bars that were predominantly black, white, and Asian; bars that were just experimenting with karaoke and bars that had retained it for years; bars where it worked and bars where it didn't. I've tried to accommodate the multiple perspectives that collide within any karaoke bar, including those of devotees and dilettantes, veterans and novices, lovers and loathers. I've tried to register karaoke's movements through time and space, attending to its evolution both overall and within certain bars and scenes, and to performers' and emcees' movements between bars and scenes (efforts aided by the length of the project and by my own relocations over its course). And, rather than fight karaoke's infiltration of every corner of my life, I've sought to accept it and, as method actors say, to use it. I've read everything I could find on karaoke, subscribed to newsletters and Internet lists, tracked its appearances in films and TV shows, and talked about it with anyone who was willing. I've dragged friends, relatives, colleagues, and students to karaoke bars, and treated them (and myself) as "subjects" as much as anyone else. Periodically, as research has required and sanity permitted, I've allowed this innocent pastime to become the prime mover of my world, to the point where I see it in everything and everything in it.

If ethnography is ever to work through people's everyday experience of media and popular culture, it will require not only new practices of fieldwork but new forms of writing. Writing ethnography shouldn't be "a mopping-up activity at the end of a research project," but "a way of 'knowing'—a method of discovery and analysis."[58] Rather than presenting "data" as supposedly unreconstructed raw material for theoretical explanation, I try to muster a voice that dramatizes the meanings and feelings that run through a typical karaoke night. This means dwelling on the concrete and the particular, using stories to convey some of the processual, improvised quality of events. It means using academic jargon sparingly and everyday idioms liberally, being "respectful of vernacular accounts of experience."[59] It means letting in the world, pursuing far-flung metaphors and unlikely connections, erring on the side of muddle-headedness rather than simple-mindedness.[60]

Most of all, it means writing with passion. In their efforts to legitimate the study of popular culture, to take it up coolly and shake off its "fannish" associations, scholars often struggle to set aside their own and others' feelings about their objects of study. But pop culture, especially pop music, is all about feelings. It's "culture that sticks to your skin," culture that's immediate and visceral, that attracts and repels in ways that make traditional modes of academic writing seem pale.[61] Academics, deep thinkers by trade, have a knee-jerk tendency to hone in on meanings and messages, but popular music is not primarily a medium for transmitting messages and conveying meanings. It is, for many of us, a way of feeling and experiencing, an apparatus for organizing desire and finessing everyday life.[62] Like many pop music fans (and many karaoke performers), I can't claim much formal understanding of music. I took a few piano lessons in junior high school; my teacher had bad breath and I never got past "Papa Haydn." My ignorance of the classical canon is shameful, and as I get older, even the pop releases seem divided between bands I've never heard of and bands I'm no longer interested in. But I know what it's like to get so spooked by a song on a car radio that I have to pull over, and I know what it's like to get so caught up in a karaoke performance that I forget where I am. I'm for a mode of ethnographic writing that emulates the raptures of music itself, that aspires (even if against hope) to the sense of living-from-within music that can be found in novels like Nick Hornby's *High Fidelity* and Roddy Doyle's *The Commitments*, or in the best rock criticism.[63]

Some scholars fear that letting emotions into research will promote solipsism and compromise the task of social analysis. "Immersed in their culture, half in love with their subject," Tania Modleski writes of audience-oriented critics like Lawrence Grossberg, "they sometimes seem unable to achieve the proper critical distance from it."[64] Yet loving a subject doesn't preclude being critical about it, any more than a concern with feelings precludes a concern with social theory. "Even when they appear most subjective," writes Renato Rosaldo, "thought and feeling are always culturally shaped and influenced by one's biography, social situation, and historical context."[65] People's feelings aren't neatly cordoned off somewhere in isolation from their social selves; they're at the very heart of the dramas through which social processes get played out. If you want to understand how the media channel our subjectivities into society's dominant forms, consider how certain songs feel more "natural" to you as a karaoke performer, how some songs trip off your tongue while others fall flat. If you want to glimpse the consequences of living in a society where musical performance by nonprofessionals verges on the deviant, consider the anguish so many karaoke customers go through over the simple decision to sing. In important ways, a full theoretical accounting of such processes *requires* some attention to feelings.[66] I'm less interested in "building" or "generating" theory than in writing in a way that embodies and enacts theory, makes it tangible and usable. Just as good karaoke can bring old songs back to life, so good ethnography can bring old theory back to life.

And yet, ethnography ought not to proceed solely in the service of theory. Theory can never fully encompass the fullness of meaning in social life, as "the object of study always exceeds its analytic circumscription."[67] In my travels, I've seen people sit half paralyzed, staring at a stack of slips on which they've scribbled song titles, unable to get up and hand one to the emcee. I've seen people get so choked up by their own performances that they're unable to continue. I've seen them descend from the stage and hug their friends as if they'd just won the lottery or survived a plane crash. I've seen them sheepishly slip emcees $50 bills to let them sing one more song. I've seen bartenders grumble under their breath while a few stragglers, refusing to leave, sing into the night. I've seen total strangers belt out tunes with all their being to rooms that were empty except for myself. I can't claim to understand all this, but that doesn't rule it out for discussion. Every story should have its loose ends, if only to leave room for further stories.

WHAT WOULD YOU THINK
IF I SANG OUT OF TUNE?

W hen karaoke's promoters claim that "anyone can do it," they're not just selling their wares. They're echoing a sentiment shared by partisans of so many revolutions in popular music, from rockabilly to punk, rhythm and blues to rap. It's a sentiment eloquently expressed by ethnomusicologist John Blacking, "There is so much music in the world that it is reasonable to suppose that music, like language and possibly religion, is a species-specific trait in man [*sic*]." Or, by the famous injunction that appeared in an early punk fanzine under illustrations of finger positions on the neck of a guitar, "Here's one chord, here's two more, now form your own band."[1]

Indeed, one of karaoke's greatest pleasures is encountering all the people who have never had voice training, who have never sung publicly, who may swear up and down that they "can't sing"—and who are, in fact, perfectly wonderful singers. People who may work with you or live with you, who may have been right in front of you all along.

Everything about karaoke seems calculated to convince prospective performers that it's a no-risk proposition. Emcees solicit applause before, after, and often during every performance. Audiences are encouraged to be, and typically are, almost ridiculously supportive. There's a place here for everyone, you're told. Ability doesn't matter. Anyone can do it.

Not Anyone Can Do It

Donna is a thirty-nine-year-old single mom living outside Albany. She's a music lover, the sort whose daily round is organized by pop songs. At her data processing job, she says, the only thing that sustains her is her Walkman. Flipping through the three thousand titles in the Tally-Ho Pub's karaoke menu, she knows more songs than I know, and I know a lot. Donna isn't shy. When I do Marshall Crenshaw's "Someday, Someway," she joins me onstage and dances magnificently. And despite her thick New York patois, she isn't afraid of her voice. She recalls that when she worked in telemarketing, men would ask her on dates just from hearing her on the phone.

Donna has all the makings of a karaoke performer. All, that is, except one. She can't sing. Or so she claims.

"Everybody can sing," I say.

"Not me," she insists. "If I get up there and sing, I'll drive this crowd right out of here."

She's jotting down titles from the song menu for her friends to perform, enjoying the secondhand satisfactions of a playlist arranger. I look over her list: TLC's "Waterfalls," Janet Jackson's "Escapade," Salt-N-Pepa's "Let's Talk About Sex."

"How's this one go?" I ask her, knowing full well how it goes.

"*Let's talk about sex, baby, let's talk about you and me*," she sings, no worse than dozens of performers I've seen.

"That's singing," I say. "That's called singing."

She laughs. "I don't think so!"

"Do you like to sing?" I ask her. "Do you ever sing?"

Her response is one I've heard from many people who know about karaoke, who are intrigued by it, but who categorically refuse to try it. "Sure I sing," she says. "When I'm alone."

Being "Unmusical"

Few would deny that music's meaning and value—that music itself—originates in social life. Music, like language, is both seed and fruit of human contact. So what's to be made of the fact that, for many in our society, some of our most active, creative musical moments—those moments when we break out in song—take place in solitude? We sing in the shower or in the car. At the traffic light, we catch the person in the next car staring at us, and we clam up. Despite every reassurance from karaoke emcees (or ethnomusicologists, or do-it-yourself punk rockers) that music is a universal human capacity, we run and hide to exercise this capacity. We all *do* sing yet remain convinced that we *can't* sing; a logical contradiction that becomes, for many of us, an experiential given.

Every attempt to extend music making runs up against the widespread belief that "musicality" is an innate gift that some people have and others don't.[2] Musicians refer to a singer's voice as her "instrument," as if it were something as solid and self-evident as a horn or a woodwind. And indeed, for many people, "I can't sing" becomes an unproblematic description of a physical handicap—no different from "I'm nearsighted" or "I have a trick knee." Such self-appraisals often can be traced to early childhood experiences: a grade-school music teacher's offhand insult, a failed bid for the glee club. The prescription such people internalize is *not* to sing, *not* to make music—at least, not publicly—thus rounding out a cycle that assures their "unmusicality."

As fate would have it, now and then, these souls who are convinced they can't sing find themselves in a spot where they just might prove themselves wrong. Maybe they're dragged there by friends, maybe they're out for a drink and have no idea what they're getting into, or maybe they're just curious. They watch intently, fascinated and repelled. They laugh, then frown, then recoil. "No, no," they cry, if someone suggests they try it. They'd just as soon go skydiving or volunteer for a root canal. You can see it in their eyes: they fear karaoke.

The only ones who may fear it more are those who are convinced that they *can* sing.

Voices Breaking

Tommy Starr, his Christian name, and a consummate stage name. A former amateur boxer, his white t-shirt and jeans stretch tightly over his trim, muscular frame. With his light brown skin and short, curly black hair, he resembles the handsome pop singer Jon Secada—except for his fractured nose, which, like Brando's, only makes him more striking. I met Tommy on a Monday at the Cherry Lounge in South Jersey—a cramped, dingy place with poor sound that draws only a handful of singers. He sat with three other people, his girlfriend and another couple, all of whom seemed content to watch him perform. Tommy stood out effortlessly, caressing ballads by George Benson and James Ingram with his luscious tenor. Men in the audience cheered; women screamed.

I complimented him after his take on Ingram's "Just Once," and we started talking. He moved quickly from his career (managing a rental center) to his former avocation (boxing) to his new passion, singing. He always sensed he could sing, he said, but never did so publicly until he discovered karaoke. He was taking lessons now. His dream was to appear on the TV amateur hour *Star Search*. I told him about Saturday night at Chollett's, one of my favorite karaoke spots in the area, where the crowds are huge, the song selection seemingly infinite, and the sound professional quality. As he left, he pointed at me and said, "See ya Saturday," and I wasn't sure if I was being addressed as a friend or a fan.

Such late-night, barroom promises usually amount to nothing, but Tommy is there at Chollett's the following Saturday. He greets me with a ready smile, remembers my name. His entourage is streamlined tonight, just his girlfriend, Hillary, a tall, pretty blonde who acts as Tommy's sounding board and moral supporter. She peruses the song menu with him, now and then suggesting, "That one would be good for you." Tommy's easy manner can't hide the fact that he really cares about this. He sweats over the song list for a good half an hour before settling on Marvin Gaye's "Sexual Healing." During our long wait to perform, he regales me with pointers on vocal technique: sing from the chest, let your breath out slowly, don't hold the mike too close.

Finally, our turns come up. I do U2's "Mysterious Ways" and mangle it until it's almost unrecognizable and I'm almost voiceless. Bombing always leaves me a little deflated, but I'm so used to it by now—so acutely aware of my limits—that it hardly matters. Tommy's up right after me. The emcee introduces him as "a new face here," and people turn to check him out. Sometimes, when you get onstage and hear your song's opening chords, you can tell that you're doomed before you even open your mouth. From the look on his face, Tommy can tell very soon after he opens his— and so can everyone else.

"*Bay-aay-aay-bee-eee*." Gaye's melody extends to heights where most of us mortals, Tommy included, become prone to nosebleeds. So he breaks off, and asks the emcee to restart the song in a lower key. The crowd is getting restless. The emcee pushes some buttons and tries again, but it's no use. As each high note approaches, Tommy's face strains, and his voice breaks like a pubescent boy's. I anticipate the breaks and feel myself inwardly cringing: "*Whenever* (gasp) *bloo-ooo tee-eeerdrops are fallin'* . . . *I just get on the telephone and* (gasp) *caa-all yoo-ooo up, bay-bee*."

Most of the crowd has turned back to their conversations, or just turned away. It seems like only two of us are left watching: me, standing in back, and Hillary, standing a few feet in front of me, her arms folded. Tommy struggles through the song and descends to quiet applause. I offer the obligatory pleasantries—you did fine, that was a tough song, et cetera—but they sound hollow even to me. There doesn't seem to be much more to talk about, and pretty soon, Tommy and Hillary leave.

Voice and Face

In karaoke, the conviction that you've failed by purely formal standards of vocal competence can bring on all the symptoms of a personal, even moral, lapse. You might feel guilty, as though you've presented yourself falsely and been caught red-handed. You might feel confused, uncertain about where you stand or where to go from there. You might feel dejected, perhaps keen to crawl into a nice, warm casket.

Singing ability can come to anchor a performer's *face*, the image pressed upon her by her own and others' efforts within the moment. Erving Goffman notes that "a person . . . cathects his [*sic*] face; his 'feelings' become attached to it."[3] Vocal competence can come to mandate a performer's temporary sense of self; those who sing well tend to feel well, and to evince well-being. Henry Kingsbury's observations regarding conservatory students' investments in their competencies could as easily describe many karaokists, "The association . . . between their musicality and their self-image was not unlike the link between a teenager's self-confidence and sense of sexual attractiveness."[4]

Audience members, also, have an investment in the success of performances. The performer's image of herself as a skilled vocalist and audience members' images of themselves as supportive listeners are mutually dependent. Because loss of face tends to be contagious, maintenance of face is a collective effort.[5] Sometimes this machinery hums along magnificently, regardless of performers' empirical competencies. There are bars where nary a performer can hit the broad side of a note. Passers through may sit in back, snickering, wincing, or scratching their heads. Yet a cluster of regulars stands in front, admiring and applauding and sustaining one another.

Other times, this face-saving pact between performer and audience dissolves. A performer may lose face even as others strain to help her preserve it. Another may maintain copious face even when others feel she should rightfully have forfeited it. And now and then, a performer may move along mindlessly even as the disparity between what others think of her and what she thinks they think of her widens into a perilous chasm, as in this story recounted by an emcee:

> The girl was absolutely horrible. I mean, she screamed, and it was horrible. Well, a woman who was there told the girl as a joke that she was a talent agent, and that she liked her singing. And she said, "Would you sing this song for me? It's my favorite song and I want you to do it." And we were even running low on time and the girl insisted, "This talent agent wants to hear me sing this song! Let me sing!" And people had said, "Don't let that girl back up there." Well, when she got up there, people took napkins and stuffed them in their ears, and walked around with these napkins sticking out of their ears. This girl was completely oblivious to it. She was so into what she was doing and where that other woman was, she completely ignored that anyone was ridiculing her.

Such incidents give warning that in karaoke, devastating aesthetic failures also can be devastating personal failures. It's at these moments, when an individual has become a laughingstock and yet remains "completely oblivious," that hidden feelings have the potential to break out into the open and genuinely hurt someone.

No One Can Do It

In karaoke bars, then, your sense of self can come to hinge quite precariously on your singing success. And yet it's hard to think of any place where you'd less want anything to hinge on your success. Don't be fooled by emcees' cheerful avowals that karaoke is easy; in the words of one of the more capable singers I've encountered, "It's the rawest form of performing you can do."

The power of public performers can be gauged by their ability to dictate the framework of their performances. Top Hollywood actors, we often are reminded in the entertainment news, can "green-light" their projects and have entire scripts and series written around them. So, too, famous singers (and famous people who feel inclined to sing) can have their background music tailored to their competencies and their characters. The right recorded backdrop can flatter even the narrowest voice, as is proven, for instance, by Ringo Starr's many hits. As Steve Jones writes, "The ability to record sound is power over sound."[6]

Now, imagine that you're a first-time karaoke performer, and consider the scope of your power. Though you have thousands of songs to choose from, bear in mind that the songs on the list were recorded in a studio in Seymour, Tennessee, or El Segundo, California, or some other place that's light years away, and that the musicians who recorded the songs don't know a thing about you and couldn't care less if you're a contralto or a soprano. These musicians have recorded each song in a particular key, and you have no way of knowing the key of the song you're pondering in advance. The song list doesn't tell you. The emcee can't tell you. ("They ask us that often, 'What key is it in?'" says one emcee. "We don't know what key it's in.") And even if someone could tell you, if you're like most performers (myself included), it wouldn't mean much to you anyway.

Maybe you've got a certain tune in mind, an old favorite of yours. Be warned, though, that in karaoke your competencies bear no necessary relation to your tastes. Or maybe you're considering a tune that sounds good when you sing along with it on the radio. In this case, be warned that the key of the karaoke version bears no necessary relation to that of the original recording. ("Like 'Waiting For a Girl Like You,'" one performer grumbles, "I can sing it great on the radio, but the karaoke version of it is in a weird key, and I can't quite find it in my voice.") Also, be warned that there is a world of difference between singing along with a song and singing the song yourself.

You might invent little tricks in an effort to control your fate. You might, like one performer I know, convince the emcee to let you screen your songs privately with the aid of his headphones before performing them publicly (though this is discouraged, since it interferes with the show). Or you might, like another performer, exploit the risks taken by your fellow volunteers, holding your hands over your ears and singing their songs to yourself until you come upon one that you think you can do (though you'll have to wait until the following week to do it, since there's an unofficial rule against doing a song that's already been done that evening).

If you're lucky, whatever song you cast your lot on will land squarely within your vocal range. For me, this occurs about one time in five. Many performers do better than I do, and some do worse. I know only a few regular performers who never sing a song out of their range. They've worked up large collections of karaoke discs that they screen at home and get emcees to play for them at bars. (Feel free to follow their lead; the discs are available for about thirty dollars each at most music stores.)

If the song you choose is not in your range, you have two choices. You can either sing it in the key it's in and leave the impression that you have no voice, or sing it in your preferred key and leave the impression that you have no ear. After shredding my vocal cords on far too many high notes, I've come to prefer the second alternative. Be advised that this option requires a degree of confidence. It requires you to stay stubbornly off-key even as many others present sing insistently on key—trying to bring you into line, assuming you're unaware of your error.

Leaving the stage before finishing your song is not an option. On those rare occasions when performers do so, they affirm their failure all too decisively and sacrifice the token applause that greets even the most miserable performances. Choosing an out-of-range song is like dressing wrong for a party—you may realize it very early, but there's not much you can do about it. You may become so hoarse that you find yourself nearly incapable of uttering another lyric. You may reach the point where, watching the members of your audience hightail it to the bar or the bathroom, you envy them rather than resent them. Still, you're expected to go the distance.

You may attempt to take advantage of the "pitch control" feature that many karaoke machines advertise. Regular performers can often be heard whispering something like "two notches down" to the emcee as they approach the stage, meaning that the key should be brought down two microtones from the backing track's default key. By experimenting with the same song at different levels week after week, you may hold out hope of calibrating it to your voice. Be advised that this function remains rather primitive on most machines. The track's key is usually varied by changing its *speed*, so you may end up with what sounds like a 45-rpm record played at 33 rpm, without any noticeable change in key.

After many trials and almost as many errors, you may build up a repertoire of a few songs within your compass. Interestingly, regular performers who lack voice training have an advantage in this regard over trained singers who lack experience in karaoke. Trained singers know how their voices are classified in objective terms, but don't know how their voices will jibe with karaoke's enigmatic backing tracks. Indeed, many trained singers are reluctant to try karaoke for fear of injuring either their voices or their egos. By contrast, regular karaoke performers may not know their objective range, but they build up a practical knowledge of their range of texts. (Do not, however, expect a song you've perfected at one bar necessarily to work at others. The emcees may use different brands of software, and two or three different software companies may have produced the song in entirely different keys.)

To have a little collection of songs that you know you can do lends you a tactical advantage. You can open with them to establish your competence (performers often refer to their best tunes as "icebreakers"), or fall back upon them when you've thrown it in doubt. In the minds of your fellow patrons, these songs become identified with you no less than with their original artists. "Once you get a hit," one performer observes, "it's not only a hit with you, it's like a hit on the radio."

And yet, like hits on the radio, you'll find that your own hits have a limited shelf life. "You get bored with the same old stuff," says another performer. "You figure that people are tired of hearing you do the same song all the time." When you're operating in a social world as small as the typical karaoke bar, with a catalogue of possible expressions as large as the typical karaoke list, it's common courtesy to modify your repertoire now and then. Yet every time you hazard a new number, you're back to square one.

Throughout this ordeal, you're likely to feel vaguely troubled about how good you are and how good you ought to be, particularly in comparison to the recording artists whose voices you displace. The anxiety of influence looms large in karaoke. The very absence of the familiar star's voice seems to summon you to fill it in. You find yourself instinctively reproducing the most convoluted cadenzas and subtle sighs of the original recordings without any prompting from the lyric monitor. You may prepare for your performances by studying the originals; you may even (like one performer I met) listen to tapes of your performances back-to-back with the originals to evaluate yourself. As among the amateur rock musicians observed by H. Stith Bennett, it may seem to you that your "ability to copy music [is] the exhibition of [your] technical accomplishment."[7]

As Bennett and others will inform you, however, the task you've set for yourself is "humanly impossible."[8] In this age of tape splicing and digital recording—when popular songs are no longer documents of real-time performances but assemblages of the best moments of many performances—not even the stars themselves can replicate the sounds of their recordings in live performance.[9] And you are attempting to do so with inferior equipment and minimal preparation.

It would seem, then, that karaoke is impossible. Not only can't "anyone" do it; no one can.

Do It Anyway

I've done my best to provide every good reason not to try karaoke: the pervasive assumption that singing skill is uncommon and cannot be taught, the damage that a failed performance can inflict upon one's sense of self, the many technical obstacles to virtuosity. For the remainder of the chapter, I'll make the case for trying it anyway.

Up until this point, I've abided by a particular vocabulary to describe singing. I've distinguished performers' voices based on accuracy, flexibility, and purity; I've characterized them as on- or off-key, broad or narrow in range, clear or distorted. These are the terms of traditional voice training, terms that most people understand and accept.

Alternatively, we might begin by regarding song as an extension of speech. The distinction between speaking and singing, while universally recognized, is hard to define empirically. Singing is, as one music educator notes, "primarily elongation of the vowels and extension of the pitch inflections commonly heard in the speaking voice."[10] Yet while we've come to see that any language engenders innumerable ways of speaking, and that even apparently incorrect utterances can be appropriate within certain communities and contexts,[11] we're not always willing to grant the same variability to song. Our understanding of singing as a form of competence can blind us to its flexibility as a means of expression.

Simon Frith writes: "In songs, words are the signs of a voice. A song is always a performance and song words are always spoken out—vehicles for the voice. . . . Song words, in short, work as speech, as structures of sound that are direct signs of emotion and marks of character."[12] If songs work as speech, then singing voices should be potentially as diverse as speaking voices. Against the conventional vocal standards of range and intonation, attack and release, diction and breath control, we might come to value a singing voice for the cogency and force with which it communicates.

This is, in fact, how many of the popular singers whom karaoke performers emulate beg to be regarded. Most popular songs seem inferior when judged on traditional musicological grounds,[13] and popular singers rarely measure up to the standards of classical vocal training. In the estimation of an operatic critic like Robert Rushmore, Elvis Presley had only "a passing baritone range with a pleasing quality in the middle compass"; Bruce Springsteen's songs "rely totally on the tonic, dominant and subdominant chords and scarcely range an octave."[14]

What popular singers, especially rock singers, *do* have over opera *prime donne* is access to the everyday "signs of emotion and marks of character" extolled by Frith; those shouts, moans, wails, and squeals that, while stifled by classical training, are vital components in the expressive repertoire of the human voice. Frith continues, "[Rock's] sound effects are those of daily life. The sound questions raised are nonmusical: Why do we respond the way we do to a baby's cry, a stranger's laugh, a loud, steady beat? Because so much of rock music depends on the social effects of the voice, the questions about how rock's effects are produced are vocal, not musicological. What makes a voice haunting? sexy? chilling?"[15] From this angle, the lack of formal training among popular singers and their listeners does not handicap them, but simply forces them to fall back on more quotidian faculties.[16] "Ignorance of how their music makes sense certainly puts no limit on a rock audience's appreciation. All that needs to be taken for granted is the common experience of desire, hope, fear."[17]

Experienced karaoke performers sense that each of the songs they select bears its own marks of character and poses its own challenges and opportunities. As one performer states, "You want to do songs that you can 'cover.' I mean, if I'm listening to the radio in my car, I'll sing along with whatever is playing. But when I'm here, I want to sing a song where I can sound like the artist." As a result, song choices often are based on a subtle feeling of affinity—of a kindred voice and sensibility—with the original vocalist. A performer who sounds all wrong emulating the crystal-clear tones of Karen Carpenter or Maureen McGovern may be right at home belting out Janis Joplin. Another may struggle with Elton John's and Billy Joel's vocal gymnastics, only to find his niche in Lou Reed's flat murmur. For my part, I've found that some of my best karaoke covers are of puppy-dog crooners like the Everly Brothers, the Beach Boys, and the Fleetwoods (thus forcing me to come to terms with my own mawkishness. More on this reflexive self-monitoring through performance in the next chapter.).

Pop songs and stars, then, are conduits as well as exemplars of public culture; they don't merely impose their voices on listeners, but make their voices available. The presence of songs from singers as diverse as Bob Dylan, Tina Turner, and Joe Cocker on karaoke lists sanctions every Dylanesque whiner, Turneresque screecher, and Cockeresque grunter to take the stage. In karaoke, pop stars become direct facilitators of musical participation; those vocal deviants whom the mass audience has granted a pulpit, in some sense, return the favor.

Three More Ways to Do It

The diversity of popular music sets a mood for karaoke and, at its best, infuses it with a rare spirit of tolerance and playfulness. Contrary to the fears of many neophytes, there is no one right way to do karaoke. Experienced performers routinely move and involve audiences even while transgressing dominant vocal standards. As I'll show in the following sections, they do so by communicating in ways their audiences can relate to, by conjuring a feeling of hangdog humility or irreverent foolishness or careless spontaneity. I begin with a personal story.

"I Don't Know These Words!": The Self-Deprecator

The reformed synagogue that my family attended when I grew up was a center for social interaction and cultural continuity. Thankfully, it was not a rigorous inculcator of language and doctrine. In seven years of attending Hebrew school, my brothers and I learned little of the alphabet and less of the language. For our Bar Mitzvahs, Rabbi Agin tape-recorded our *Haftorahs*, the excerpts of the Hebrew Bible we had to recite. We would take these tapes home and listen to them and repeat them, and the rabbi would drill us every week. Though we didn't understand the words we were singing, they mattered deeply to us. This was an exercise in mnemonics. It was like "Simon," that board game we played in which you had to push the buttons in sequence as they lit up one by one. Also like Simon, there were winners and losers.

My youngest brother, Ken, was Bar Mitzvahed in September, which meant that his *Haftorah* was one of the longest of the year. It filled four pages in his study book and almost a full side of his tape. Ken wasn't much of a student in Hebrew school or any other school, but he somehow took to the task. He'd sit up on his bunk bed with his tape recorder, listening and repeating, and rewinding and listening again, taking in the strange speech bit by bit.

The day of his Bar Mitzvah arrived, and Ken put in a splendid showing. Even Uncle Max, the orthodox cantor, praised the little mensch for his command of scripture. My parents were hopeful that Ken's success might spill over to his school performance, perhaps even spark an interest in temple services. Instead, Ken returned to his cassette player, not with Torah tapes, but with tapes of rap music given to him by his best friend, Melvin "Beh-beh" Watson. Instead of Rabbi Agin, his new tape tutors were the Sugarhill Gang, Grandmaster Flash, and Run-D.M.C. Again, Ken sat up on his bunk, listening and repeating and rewinding.

Before long, Ken could rattle off any rap on demand, chapter and verse. They'd flow osmotically in and out of his everyday speech. (Dad, driving us to school: "This new clutch is tricky." Ken: "IT'S TRICKY-TO-ROCK-A-RHYME-TO-ROCK-A-RHYME-THAT'S-RIGHT-ON-TIME-IT'S-TRICKAAAY!!!") Sometimes he'd just sit with a glazed look, unraveling rhymes under his breath like some autistic homeboy. My brother Larry and I marveled at this miniature, melanin-deficient Melle Mel—as did kids of all persuasions, at least in our little town.

Then Ken went away to college, and the first white rap group, the Beastie Boys, came out. And Ken said, "That shoulda been me." And Ken went to graduate school, and the dopest white rap group, 3rd Bass, came out. And even though Ken thought 3rd Bass was fresh, he still said, "That shoulda been me." And Ken started his career in social work, and the phoniest white rapper, Vanilla Ice, came out. And even though Ken knew Vanilla Ice was a sucker, he still said, "That shoulda been me." And nowadays, every white boy from the suburbs reckons himself a "gangsta."

So when I bring Ken to Mickey's in Albany for one of his first karaoke outings, and leafing through the song list, he comes upon the Sugarhill Gang's "Rapper's Delight"—the first U.S. rap hit and the first rap Ken ever learned—there's no doubt what his choice will be. There's something to prove here. This is *old school*, from *back in the day*. And although he's not sure what toll the years have taken on his verbal magic, he's willing to find out. Besides, there's a lyric monitor here to fall back on. Waiting his turn, Ken quietly rehearses, mouthing the words a little less assuredly than he did fifteen years ago.

Ken's name is called. He gets up in front of the mostly white rockers at Mickey's and starts rapping. His opening is mesmerizing. He whizzes through the hip-hip-hops and bang-bang-boogies like an exquisite machine. He summons the crowd in the open, inviting terms of early rap: *"I am the Wonder Mike and I'd like to say hello, to the black and the white, the red and the brown, the purple and yellow!"* The rockers in the audience call back, gettin' funky.

Then, about two minutes in, something awful happens. Ken launches into the third verse: *"I'm the C-A-S-AN-the-O-V-A."* But different words appear on the screen: *"I'm Imp the Dimp, the ladies' pimp."* "Rapper's Delight," which may be the only rap ever recorded that's as long as Ken's *Haftorah,* has been edited for karaoke. The version on the lyric monitor has jumped over several verses and landed at a point that's hard to situate. His template ruptured, poor Kenny looks as though he's been dropped in the middle of the south Bronx circa 1980, a clueless, thirteen-year-old wanna-be.

Ken silently scans the screen for a familiar lyric to get his bearings. But silence screams in karaoke. People who hadn't been watching turn to see what's wrong; those who had been watching look away in pain. So he tries to fake it, but the words roll by too fast: *"That shock the house . . . you do the freak, spank . . ."* Reduced from a million-dollar man to a five-dollar boy in a matter of seconds, Ken announces desperately, "I don't know these words!"

"Just read 'em!" comes a voice from the crowd.

Ken lowers his six-foot, two-inch frame and squints into the lyric monitor. "I can't!" he sputters.

The folks at Mickey's aren't ones to ignore a cry for help. They're the kind who'd offer a hand if you got your car stuck in the Albany snow, even if it meant getting their feet wet. Or who'd lend a voice if you were stuck in the middle of a song, even if they could only mitigate your discomfort by sharing in it. So the rockers join in, tripping through the rap and collectively producing some semblance of a narrative. *"We're a treacherous trio, we're the serious joint."* And Ken, lifted by their efforts, recovers his rhythm and takes the lead. *"She said she's heard stories and she's heard fables, that I'm vicious on the mike and the turntable."* And when the hook line comes around, the line of "Rapper's Delight" that most everyone knows, we all shout out, *"Ho-tel, mo-tel, Ho-li-day Inn!"*

Ken never quite regains the mastery of his opening lines. His memory has compressed the script very differently from the karaoke software producers. Nonetheless, he gets through the performance, he engages the audience, and he's rewarded with healthy applause and some slaps on the back. What's more, the folks at Mickey's thereafter address him by name, they kid him about his troubles onstage—they like him.

Aside from the natural appeal of watching a sibling squirm, what intrigued me about Ken's performance was the metamorphosis of the vaunting persona who took the stage, into the vulnerable one who eventually won the audience's approval. It seemed that his very loss of composure ("I don't know these words!") was the act that precipitated his recovery. Such "one-down" moves—excuses, apologies, disclaimers—are common face-saving strategies in everyday interaction,[18] but tend to be suppressed in onstage performance. (One public speaking textbook counsels emphatically, *"Never place on your listeners the burden of sympathy for you as a speaker."*)[19] In karaoke, though, the crowd's sense of inclusion and its understanding of the severity of the task foster a readiness to accept self-deprecators and even to root for them. Like Cameron Diaz muddling through "I Just Don't Know What to Do With Myself" in *My Best Friend's Wedding*, the self-deprecator knows she's bad (as does everyone else) but wins the crowd over through sheer pluckiness.

And so performers preface their songs with coy disavowals, "I don't know if I can sing this," or "Don't expect us to be good." Or they signal their frustration with their execution by frowning, shaking their heads, and critiquing themselves, "Can't do it, can't do it." Or they leave the stage audibly muttering, "That was hard," or "That was awful." Although such gestures and comments digress from performers' song scripts, they often seem no less scripted than the songs themselves. They are gambits in the sort of corrective process triggered by face-threatening events of all kinds.

The audience, too, plays a role in this process. I found that whenever I complained about my performances, no matter how atrocious they were, others would reassure me. Audience members' acceptance of a performer's apologies seems to absolve them no less than the apologies absolve the performer. As one emcee states, "If somebody says, 'That was terrible,' you sort of have this obligation to say, 'Oh, no, it was good,' even though you know it stunk." Along with obligations, though, such moments present the crowd with opportunities, to put karaoke's "anyone can do it" creed into action, and to feel a complicity in that creed. Often, as a performer publicly confesses that she's a second-rate singer (and thus signals that she's aware of it), a collective sigh of relief seems to emanate from the crowd. They understand that there are a hundred other good reasons to want to sing.

These little dramas of supplication and expiation need have little to do with anyone's true feelings. Crowd members may pardon a performance even when they "know it stunk," and performers may beg the crowd's pardon even when they're inwardly self-assured. Hence, a performer with whom I once sang a duet announced to the audience before we started, "I have a cold—I won't sound good tonight." She then turned away from the mike and whispered to me, "I say that every time." Another performer gleefully recounted how he'd gone to a strange bar and performed all the songs he'd rehearsed and honed at his regular bar. As he'd taken the stage, he'd adopted the demeanor of a novice, inspecting the equipment confusedly and asking, "What's this thing? How does this work?" His fumblings thus composed a performance in themselves, a fabricated show of humility of which he was secretly quite proud.

"This Could Get Ugly": The Clown

If Laurel and Hardy were reincarnated as a couple of northeast Philly goombahs, they might look something like Ed and Dave. Ed's the big one, sporting a sweat suit circa 1970, a greased-back scalp, and a slightly demented smile. Scrawny Dave wears a t-shirt, jeans, stringy hair, and an expression that is not all there.

Ed spits into the mike to test it out. "So I'm in line at the bank," he says. "I got my tongue up this . . . " He breaks off just before the sordid payoff of his Andrew Dice Clay joke, and his friends in the audience chuckle.

"He's up here doing the Diceman," announces the emcee. "This could get ugly." As if to stifle Ed, the emcee quickly spins the disc they've requested, "You've Lost That Lovin' Feelin'." It doesn't take long to discern why whoever they're singing to has lost that lovin' feelin'.

As the song begins, Dave suddenly emerges from his trance and takes the lead, such as it is. He's the one who howls the tune like a stray mutt, miles off-key and off-tempo, laughing and waving his arms ridiculously. He's the one who, midway through the song, quits singing and starts whacking his partner over the head with his mike. He's the one who unceremoniously drops his mike and walks offstage as the last chorus ends—followed closely by Ed, who announces broadly, "I ain't never singin' with him again!"

And he's the one who gets the biggest hand of the night.

The fool and the clown: deft negotiators of pratfalls, donners of lampshades, depositors of foodstuffs in oversized trousers. Orrin Klapp first noted the paradox that, though fools themselves are ridiculed, the role they perform is often prized. "The fool upsets decorum by antics and eases routine by comic relief. He also acts as a cathartic symbol for aggressions in the form of wit."[20] More than a mere scapegoat or steam valve, however, the fool can be an innovator, a source of insight and power. Barbara Babcock views clowning as a form of native theorizing, an epistemological critique. "The clown's performance . . . disrupts and interrupts customary frames and expected logic and syntax, and creates . . . an open space of questioning."[21]

In karaoke, clowning serves as a critique of the classical voice and as yet another way for participants to convince themselves that "anyone can do it." Whereas other performers fret over minor slips off-key, the clown sings wildly, shamelessly off-key. Where others maintain a solemn bearing, the clown objectifies himself with contorted postures and expressions. Rather than shore up prevailing standards of song performance, the clown overturns and relativizes them. As one emcee states: "If you get up there and act like, 'I'm being a clown and I want you to know it,' then they'll treat you like, 'Hey, this guy's funny! He was wonderful that way!'"

While some performers are clownish from the outset, others seem to have clownishness thrust upon them. The same emcee continues, "I have seen people get up to do songs, they start out serious but it's just not working, and they immediately go into, 'I'm doing it as a joke.'" Clowning here works as a face-saving stopgap when performers are failing. When a pair of young men try "Little Red Corvette" and find themselves unable to keep up with the words, one of them resorts to a coarse, Duranti-esque dialect that's out of joint with Prince's sexy number. This draws some laughter from the crowd and some dissipative ribbing from the emcee, "I bet you'll wake up in the morning feeling really good about doing that!"

47

Clowning has its limits. Its suitability depends on the song and it can yield diminished returns if pursued too relentlessly. Yet in karaoke, it isn't unusual for the folly to mount to the point where it dominates the event. At such times, it's the serious performer who can come to feel out of place. Consider the comments of one smooth-voiced regular karaokist, "It's the funniest thing. The singers that people seem to enjoy the most are the ones that are drunk out of their minds, acting stupid, and don't sing a note right or sing all the wrong words. It's so funny, people would rather see that sometimes than the good ones—which is just as well, because that's what makes it fun." Though she struggles to be tolerant, this performer can't hide her bewilderment that some audiences would prefer travesties of songs over faithful renderings. She is, understandably, torn between her respect for karaoke's pluralist ideal and her resentment at karaoke's demotion of her own painstakingly nurtured voice.

"It Just Popped Into My Head": The Improvisor

A well-dressed woman is doing "Midnight Train to Georgia," backed by three male friends. The division of labor recalls the hit version by Gladys Knight and the Pips, and the performers try to reproduce the call-and-response of their template. But the boys' Pips impersonation is so convincing that Gladys can't help laughing, and as she breaks up, unable to continue, her Pips go right on singing. Their backing vocals are thrust absurdly to the foreground—"*Leavin' on a midnight train! . . . Goin' back to find! . . . I know you will!*"—and the longer they continue, the more thoroughly they disable their lead singer.

It sometimes seems as though these little routines ("you be Gladys Knight, we'll be the Pips") are put together just so they can fall apart. The laughter, raised eyebrows, and fumbling for words give the impression that these are no longer performers, but real human beings appearing before us. Suddenly, their difficulties seem twice as arduous, their solutions twice as ingenious. Spontaneity has an almost magical effect in karaoke:

> I'll sing a song and a phrase will pop into my head, and I'll change the words right then and there on the spot. I was singing a song last week, "Jessie's Girl." There's a phrase in the song, he says, "*I find myself staring in the mirror all the time, wondering what she doesn't see in me.*" The next phrase says something, I don't even know what it says because I changed

the words, it just popped into my head. After "*what she doesn't see in me*,"
I said, "*Could it be that he has thirteen inches and I just have a little peewee?*"

Onstage and offstage, performers take pains to assure us that such emendations "popped into their heads." So strong is the appeal of miscarried schemes and makeshift recoveries that some performers are tempted to contrive them. Thus, a college kid doing "Jailhouse Rock" appears to be thrown off by the song's breakneck tempo and abruptly shifts to a weird hybridization of Presley's lyrics with scat-style nonsense syllables—"*Obada oobada eebada let's rock!*"—animating the whole with bowlegged, jitterbug movements. Later, he depicts his performance as an ad hoc response to a mnemonic impasse: "My friend chose the song, and the reason I improvised the way I did was because I didn't quite know all the words. . . . My high school band teacher was into the weird kind of phrases I was using. So I was like, might as well pull it out of the hat right now. 'Cause I had nowhere to turn, I didn't know the words!"

Yet the following week, he does the same song, the same scat singing, the same jitterbug dancing. His performance is improvised in the sense that it could hardly be identical to his previous one, but this is clearly a planned and polished form of improvisation. Even so, it's as good for the audience, as good for me, and evidently as good for the performer as the week before.

If karaoke performance is guided by anything like a coherent aesthetic, it's an enormously flexible aesthetic, receptive to as wide a range of voices as speech itself, and defined as much by quotidian social skills as by formal musical skills. Vocal ability is ultimately less important in karaoke than the ability to feel others out, humble oneself, laugh at oneself, think on one's feet. In this sense, karaoke recalls the many grassroots musical crusades that value the vernacular over the esoteric, social utility over individual expertise.

At a more practical level, all of this suggests that if you can cast aside your conditioned fear of your own voice, if you can remain alive to the hazards without letting them hold you back, if you can imagine a place where breaking into song is as natural as saying hello, then maybe you, too, can do it—in a karaoke bar, or anywhere else.

SINGING THE SELF

By now, you might concede that karaoke can serve as a vehicle to fine-tune one's vocal skills or overcome performance anxiety or even foster musical participation across society. Yet the notion that karaoke can be a meaningful form of individual and social expression may invite skepticism. After all, the conventional wisdom is that karaoke performers don't express much of anything, they merely sing other people's songs. Devotees hear this all the time; karaoke is nothing more than a simulacrum, one more symptom of the recession of reality in a postmodern age, in a class with blow-up dolls and televised fireplaces.

The image of karaoke performers as mere imitators has its pop music precedents. For instance, one reason many critics have denied Elvis Presley the status of a serious (self-conscious, imaginative) artist is that he did not write his own songs. Like karaoke performers, but unlike such "literate" rock musicians as Bob Dylan and John Lennon, Presley's body was his primary medium, and his artistic reputation has suffered for it.[1] Such dismissals reflect a deep-rooted predilection for composition over performance—as well as literacy over orality, mind over body—in Western cultural criticism. In Plato's *Ion*, the "rhapsode," or singer of epic poems, was characterized as a secondhand artist, an imitator of imitators of life, who was all style and no substance.[2] Until recently, much of the thinking about performance remained bound by this "text-centered" paradigm, viewing the text as the substantive basis for performance.[3]

Admittedly, performance always involves the restoration of some preexisting strip of activity. It is always "twice-behaved behavior,"[4] never a sui generis original. As Elizabeth Fine and Jean Haskell Speer argue, however, the notion of performance as mere imitation fails to appreciate its creative, meaning-making potential: "While there are certainly performances that are merely mimetic, in the Platonic sense, the best performances are mimetic in the Aristotelian sense. That is, they involve analysis and reflection . . . the art of making, as opposed to simple imitation." Fine and Speer continue, "Through performance, human beings not only present behavior . . . but they reflexively comment on it and the values and situations it encompasses. Through the myriad choices performers make, ranging from selecting and composing a text to the tone of voice or style of movement, they have the opportunity to comment on others, on a situation, and on themselves."[5]

Performance, then, can be an elaborate means of articulating personal and collective identity. Performers express their affiliations and antagonisms, their thoughts and feelings and fantasies, not by stating them outright, but by their passionate or caustic or frenetic recitations of texts. In karaoke, we can find lively evidence of people's creative engagement and emotional investment in popular songs. Studying such pop-inspired performances can be "a critical way of grasping how persons choose to present themselves, how they construct their identities, and, ultimately, how they embody, reflect, and construct their culture."[6]

Crowd Favorites

From the moment a karaoke machine is set down in a bar, you can witness its capacity to evoke a common lore and, thus, to transform a collection of individuals into a group. Participants seem to coalesce around certain performances that powerfully express their cultural affinity. It might even work at Spanky's, a Philly college bar frequented by a mostly white, well-scrubbed assortment of frat kids, jocks, and bohos. On an early September evening in 1993, the first Monday of the fall semester, one thing everyone at Spanky's seems to share is an utter disdain for the quirky bar owner's latest acquisition, a cut-rate karaoke system. The owner, Nick, is struggling to lure some performers. He and his bartenders have already sung several numbers themselves. Yet most of his collegiate patrons seem to regard Nick and his new hobbyhorse as terribly gauche; they watch him, then laugh at him, then ignore him. They only start to volunteer when Nick bribes them with free t-shirts and beer.

One likely explanation for their reluctance is that Nick has seen fit to purchase only 9 karaoke discs containing 162 songs. Of these, only about a dozen songs have been released within the past decade, the pop-conversant years of most of those present. And of these, most are teen-idol tunes loathed by college hipsters. Thus, all but a few selections hail from the hinterlands of this crowd's musical map. Their response is to remake every number as a novelty hit, a one-line joke.

When a mixed foursome does the Pointer Sisters' up-tempo dance number, "I'm So Excited," one of them sits on the stage and mumbles the words in the most unexcited voice he can muster. "*I'm so excited, and I just can't hide it,*" he states flatly, as if debating zoning provisions at a city council meeting.

When a birthday boy is forced onstage by his buddies for a go at "Sexual Healing," he transmutes Marvin Gaye's feverish mating call into a whiny wake-up call worthy of a young Jerry Lewis: "*GET UUH-UUUP! GET UUH-UUUP!*"

When three guys in polo shirts and khaki shorts grab the mikes for Elvis Presley's "Burnin' Love," their front man starts off by shouting, "Elvis was a hero to most but he never meant shit to me!" Every so often, he embellishes Presley's canonical text with bits of smart-alecky exegesis: "*Help me, I'm flamin', must be a hundred and nine*—Excuse me, but anyone who's a hundred and nine degrees is technically dead! . . . *Burnin' burnin' burnin', And nothin' can cool me*—What stupid lyrics!" He continues in the same vein after the group segues into the Beatles' "Lady Madonna": "*Listen to the music playin' in your head*—She's crazy! She's alone and she hears music! She's nuts!"

And when a short dude ascends for Elton John's "Your Song," his subtle smirk hints that he's up to something. "*It's a little bit funny, this feeling inside.*" He croons the words mawkishly, holding the mike close to his mouth, keeping a straight face. "*My gift is my song, this one's for you.*" His exaggerated sincerity already has the audience snickering, anticipating his inevitable break, which finally arrives. "*The sun's been quite bright while I wrote this song, it's for people like you who keep me turned . . . OOOAAAHH-WWNN!*" The word "on" extends into a deafening belch, sending the crowd into stitches and blowing away any inkling of seriousness in one gigantic gust.

I watch all this with mixed emotions. As a student of media audiences, I'm well aware that pop stars, songs, and genres only come to life by virtue of what their listeners make of them. Lesbian honky-tonkers bypass country music's God-and-country conservatism and value it for its tough-talking women, sentimentality, and camp potential; white fans of black rap often revel in its sexism, materialism, and self-aggrandizement, while ignoring its social and political messages.[7] I'm wise to the post-structuralist bromide that "there's no one unequivocal reading of any type of music or of particular songs."[8]

And so it's no surprise seeing the baby busters at Spanky's dancing on the graves of boomer idols like Presley and Gaye and Lennon. As its chroniclers have detailed, this is a wary, jaded, unromantic generation.[9] Presley's "Burnin' Love" and even Gaye's "Sexual Healing" must seem lukewarm to a group whose childhood limits on sexual expression were defined by tender titles like "Push, Push (in the Bush)" and "Boom, Boom, Boom (Let's Go Back to My Room)." The Beatles's "Lady Madonna," trying to make ends meet with her children at her feet, excites no great pity in kids who, having grown up with Carterite images of economic malaise and Reaganite images of welfare queens, are more worried about supporting themselves when they get out of college. Elton John's "Your Song," a heart-on-the-sleeve conceit typical of early-1970s, confessional songwriting, is unlikely to resonate with "the least emotionally demonstrative of all American generations this century."[10]

I understand all this, yet, born as I was in 1961, at the tail end of the baby boom, I find my generational defenses aroused. Where do these post-Reagan preppies get off, making a mockery of Elvis and the Beatles? Elton John cloaked himself in feathers and funky glasses so he could speak from the heart, and many of his tunes have touched me. Who are these whippersnappers to pooh-pooh him? If, according to 1970s sociologists, the cohort I grew up with suffered from an obsession with intimacy and authenticity,[11] the generation represented at Spanky's often strikes me as just the opposite: hard-shelled, severe. Their little send-ups drip with contempt. Where, I wonder, do their sympathies lie?

I'm mulling all this over when a pair of gangly boys takes the stage. They've culled something interesting from Nick's meager song list: Prince's "When Doves Cry." The record was released in the mid-1980s, around the time the national divorce rate peaked, and the sex-saturated media started spreading the word that sex could kill you. The Spanky's crew would have been in their mid-teens at the time. They're the ones who made the song a number one hit and flocked to the film that helped popularize it, *Purple Rain*, in which Prince played a cool, sexy rock singer whose parents' abuse reduces him to a confused bundle of rage, whose father's sole words of advice to him are, "Don't get married."

I've heard this song many times, yet it has always felt just out of reach. Maybe it's the music's hypnotic simplicity, or the ethereal imagery of the lyrics. The opening of the karaoke track retains the spare, ominous sound of the original: no bass line, heavy percussion, and a solitary, descending keyboard riff. The boys sing of lovers immersed in a kiss. They hardly glance at the monitor, yet they reproduce Prince's inflections, if not his timbre, flawlessly; they have his song down cold. They are smiling, but not like the earlier performers. Where the others seemed detached, these boys seem almost embarrassed. The original vocal packs even a kiss with more sensual urgency than the bluest movie, and the original vocal looms large in this performance. The song's images grow progressively surreal: a courtyard with oceans of violets, animals striking poses and sensing the lovers' heat. They express a desire that can't be consummated—a desire that's starting to break forth in the boys' quivering voices.

"How can you just leave me standing, Alone in a world that's so cold?" As the song's cool eroticism gives way to confusion and desperation, the smiles on the performers' faces turn to grimaces, and their voices turn pleading. They mimic Prince's call-and-response with himself, one of them punctuating the other's singing with plaintive highlights. Spectators scream and sway and wave their arms in unison. A boy in the corner drums frantically on a wall; a table of girls holds up lighters in tribute. In a moment of Goffmanesque downkeying,[12] these impassive college kids have suddenly gone from dabbling in karaoke to throwing themselves into it headlong.

It occurs to me that in Prince's song, as among his audience, "casual sex doesn't exist anymore."[13] Sexual contact—*human* contact—is shot through with fear and stress and power. For a generation plagued with STDs, date rape, teen pregnancy, and parental neglect, Prince's elusive rendition of interpersonal bonding must hit home. For kids coming of age in an era of diminishing expectations—regarding not only sex, but family, friendships, careers—his words must seem emblematic: maybe I'm too demanding, maybe you're never satisfied. Watching the crowd at Spanky's howl in what could be ecstasy or agony, I think of Naomi Wolf's words: "What looks from the outside like an inert generation whose silence should provoke contempt is actually a terrified generation whose silence should inspire compassion."[14]

"That's the best song to sing," I hear one of the boys say as they descend to frenzied applause, and at this bar it certainly is. In the following weeks at Spanky's, it becomes a ritual. After several indifferent recitals of moldy oldies, someone takes on "When Doves Cry" and instantly works the crowd to a fever pitch. The song becomes, in emcees' parlance, a "crowd favorite," the sort of number that can prompt a roomful of strangers to suddenly sing and move and rejoice as one. Virtually every karaoke bar has its crowd favorites. Sometimes, songs accrue this power regardless of who's singing them. The following week at Spanky's, a female foursome does "Doves" and gets a similar response. Other times, songs become inseparable from their performers. At one suburban bar partial to heavy metal, I'm told, "Joe and Jack couldn't come to Spender's without doing [Aerosmith's] 'Sweet Emotion.' The crowd would kill them."

What all crowd favorites have in common is that they seem to crystallize the experience of the people who celebrate them and, as a result, to constitute these people as members of a common culture. They function like the old hits that eternally recirculate among Elvis Presley fans via his impersonators, who often see themselves as rescuing Presley from his detractors. *Their* Elvis is the sensual, spiritual, generous, hard-working, ideal U.S. male, and they project these values with utter conviction in their performances. In protecting Presley's memory, impersonators and fans are protecting and defining themselves as a community.[15]

So it is that crowd favorites bring karaoke audiences together in passionate reenactments of their own collective litanies. The Prince song focuses the common desires and dreads felt by a college-age audience growing up at century's end. At Grand's, a happy-hour bar frequented by refugees from surrounding corporate parks, the hands-down favorite is a pair of guys in suits, ties, and sunglasses who call themselves the Business Boys and rant their way through Bachman-Turner Overdrive's "Takin' Care of Business," a hard-rock tribute to slacking off. At Madigan's, a good-ol'-boy haunt in suburban Tampa, the most popular of many popular country numbers is the bluegrass classic "Rocky Top," a nostalgic evocation of rural Appalachia that acquires new meaning when set against the New South's centerless sprawl.

Such performances serve as lodestars that crowds fix upon to situate themselves. Like the Balinese cockfight as rendered by Clifford Geertz,[16] they bring everyday experiences into focus and thereby allow audiences to see shared dimensions of their assorted lives. And though this power of articulation is more conspicuous the more celebrated the performance, it is there to some degree in every karaoke performance, in every rock or soul or country number that says, "we are rock or soul or country people."

What makes crowd favorites worth dwelling upon, aside from the fact that they are the performances crowds themselves choose to dwell upon, is that they might prompt us to rethink our bias against "imitative" performances. When I discuss karaoke with friends and colleagues, the performances they most often want to hear about—those that, in their minds, make karaoke worthwhile—are the ones in which performers freely transform hit recordings in order to communicate something original. This is, perhaps, a sign of our middle-class proclivity for elaborated, individualized discourses, in song as in speech.[17] As it happens, the songs that undergo the *least* modification in karaoke bars are, generally, the ones performers and audiences feel *most* passionate about. Performers may seem hemmed in, even oppressed, by these texts, but only because they impart so much meaning and value. If "an essential element of the sacred is its unquestionability,"[18] such songs do have something sacred about them for their celebrants—which is precisely what makes them such vital resources for self-definition.

How You Like Me Now?

It's one o'clock in the morning at Mickey's in Albany. Ten of us are left in the room, ten of us whose irresponsibility, underemployment, or sheer karaoke fanaticism allows or impels us to remain here this late on a weeknight.

The emcee, who refers to himself as "Tony Tremolo," has a sadistic streak. Like some pagan god of misrule, he sits at his controls and ponders how to shake things up for us mortals. At the moment, he's conspiring with the people at the next table who, giddy with drink and music, perversely assign one another unlikely songs to sing.

"Are you familiar with the alphabet?" Tony asks Sharon, the blond woman in the ratty Aerosmith shirt who's famous for belting out rockers by Joan Jett and Pat Benatar.

"I don't know anymore!" she sputters through her laughter.

"Well, you're gonna learn it tonight, 'cause you're doin' 'The A-B-C's'!" Her friends crack up at the prospect of Sharon ranting her way through the nursery school primer. "Just kidding!" Tony chuckles, and then he cues up the song they've really chosen for her, the Carpenters' "Top of the World."

"I hate this song!" she cries, but when the words come across the screen, she sings them—not in the loud, edgy voice of Joan Jett, but in the lilting, intimate tones of Karen Carpenter. Notwithstanding her disclaimer, this down-and-dirty rock queen's performance expresses genuine reverence for Carpenter's squeaky-clean pop classic. She seems moved by the song in spite of herself, and moves us in turn.

Tony has that naughty glimmer in his eye again. "How about a little karaoke roulette?" We groan, but he knows we love the idea. Tony broaches this little game late at night with the hard-core regular performers, after the dabblers have cleared out. "It'll give you a chance to try something brand new that you'd never think about trying."

Gary is next onstage, the biker dude in the Harley shirt and leather vest who does the raucous country numbers. But instead of cueing up the song Gary's chosen, Tony calls out to members of the audience:

"Jake, pick a number from one to seventy."

"Forty-nine!" shouts Jake. Tony pushes a button on his disc changer.

"Larry, 'A' or 'B'?"

"A," Larry answers, and Tony pushes more buttons.

"Rob, a number from one to seventeen?"

"Eight," I say. My lucky number—maybe it'll be lucky for Gary.

Maybe not. Tony rapidly punches a few more buttons and song number 49-A-8 comes up. Gary gets stuck with Bette Midler's ultra-mild, Gulf War protest song, "From a Distance." His friends roar as Gary stretches and writhes to reach the tune, which is out of his range in every possible sense.

Next up is Gary's friend Jake, who draws 17-B-13, the Bee Gees's "Jive Talkin'." Evidently, Jake missed the disco era; he's familiar with the hook line but has to fake the rest. So he modifies the song to express his mounting irritation toward his laughing buddies: "*Jive talkin', you're idi-ots, jive talkin', you are ass-holes.*"

Larry has a little better fortune. He usually does country ballads by the likes of Garth Brooks and the Eagles. Tonight his roulette draw is Lionel

Richie's "Hello," a soul ballad that's right in his key. He's skittish at first, but the melody woos him and he embraces it, putting in one of his better performances with a song he might never have chosen on his own.

Tony's roulette game puts the fear and trembling of karaoke back into these jaded veterans. Like old times, we hesitate and whine and have to be prodded to ascend the stage. Yet after playing at reluctance, we all take our turns. After groaning as our songs come up, we all muddle through. We all load up, spin the cylinder, and pull the trigger.

We do so because, while no one says as much, there's an indescribable thrill about this game for us. The randomness of the song selection provides an opportunity—and an excuse—to perform songs no one would expect us to choose, and thus to adopt voices far removed from those we normally sing in. There's a sense here that, through performance, we can "transcend the imprisoning limits of self,"[19] reinventing ourselves as disco gods or pop divas or soul balladeers, and blaming it all on the luck of the draw. And although it's intensified in karaoke roulette, this feeling of personal transformation is probably not foreign to the experience of any karaoke performer.

Closing out tonight's session is Rick, a thin, handsome, slightly goofy guy whose Led Zep t-shirt and long ponytail nicely suit his metalhead stage persona. The lord of misrule again punches in the numbers called out by the audience, and out comes Millie Small's perky, proto-reggae classic, "My Boy Lollipop." "*My boy lollipop! Ya make my heart go giddy-up!*" Rick squeals the words with a big, silly smile on his face, bobbing up and down like a little girl on an amateur hour. "*You set my heart on fire! You are my one desire!*" The song is so childish, and Rick delivers it with such childish abandon, and we all laugh incredulously and become like children for a moment.

As the tune ends and the laughter dies down, Tony says, "I hope you enjoyed that."

"Sure," says Rick.

Tony smiles. "Good," he says, "'cause I taped it." He plays the tape back, and we just about fall off our chairs.

When you're in the thick of a game of karaoke roulette, your potential for identity play seems limitless. Yet in standard karaoke, where you choose your own songs, you tend to tread more lightly. You find that social pressures come to bear on you in the form of "person-role formulas," expectations about who may act in what capacity.[20] In choosing a song, you can't help being mindful of the agreement between the original artist's demographics and your own, if only because others seem so mindful of it. Gender categories, in particular, are habitually invoked by fellow performers and emcees: "You can't do that, that's a woman's song!"

You're also likely to be sensitive to the culture of the bar, which can be as confining when you feel at odds with it as it is liberating when you feel a part of it. If you're a newcomer to the bar, you'll want to lie low for a while, observing others' performances and plotting your own. Should you notice any conspicuous generic presences or absences—a surfeit of metal, a paucity of pop—you might feel pressured to toe the line.

Regardless of the bar, you're likely to encounter an expectation that you define yourself, both personally and as a performer—in karaoke, these become one and the same. Week in and week out, performers negotiate claims to their preferred songs. It's not uncommon, as one emcee says, to be able to "look out at the crowd and name half the songs that are going to be sung." Until you stake your own claims, establishing your "signature numbers," you feel anonymous and adrift; once you establish them, others approach you more comfortably and address you with more familiarity. At one bar, patrons refer to me as "Bryan," even though I've done songs by Bryan Adams (a white, male rock singer) no more often than songs by Prince (a black soul singer) or the Go-Go's (a white female group). Still, I feel more at home at this bar than at others where people seem not to know how to classify me, leaving me in a musical and social no-person's-land.

Your conversations with fellow performers, like those between amateur rock musicians, are peppered with references to famous acts that you use to define your own and others' stage identities.[21] Consider these excerpts from an exchange of posts to the *Jolt* on-line karaoke forum between three performers who have traded tapes of each other:

> ARLENE: Connie, you sound like a combination of Bette Midler and Joni Mitchell, with a hint of Karen Carpenter.
>
> CONNIE: I know I sound a little like Karen Carpenter on my lowest notes. When I sing along with her on the radio, we blend well. . . . I think Avern sounds like Dionne Warwick.
>
> AVERN: You know what? I remember when the show "Solid Gold" first came out and I watched Dionne Warwick singing . . . and I was pre-

tending I was her. I was like twelve then and had completely forgotten about it until you guys mentioned it.

CONNIE: Avern, that's interesting, it was like an omen. Arlene, you sound like Brenda Lee. . . . Also, I hear some Janis Joplin.

ARLENE: People have told me that.[22]

As a performer, you hear such comments all the time, comments that convey others' appraisals of your performing self: "That one would be good for you," or "That one?" Significant others greet some of your choices with enthusiasm, others with quiet smirks. Certain songs you do are applauded roundly and even requested of you; others are met with dead air.

With time, you come to *feel* all right doing some tunes, all wrong doing others. There are songs you've loved for years that you suddenly hate when they're coming out of your mouth; others that you never gave a second listen to sound strangely apt coming from you. You might try to explain it to yourself and others in technical terms: the song was too high, or too low, or too fast, or too slow. But you know there's more to it, because some songs that are too high or too low feel okay, and some that are in your range feel awful. You sense something deeper: your limits as a performer, as a person.

All this casts doubt on the "fantasy" account of karaoke often touted by promoters. "For five minutes, that woman *was* Whitney Houston," one emcee reflects. "She almost started crying when she was singing, and she was so intensely into it that, for her, this was an incredible experience." At times, you might indeed feel virtually transported by a song, enjoying a fantasy-communion with the original artist, or simply surrendering to the unselfconscious, primal pleasure of your own voice. More often, though, the experience is stubbornly reflexive. You monitor your own performance, wavering "in that liminal, double-negative field where [performers] are neither themselves nor their roles."[23] Thus, the stage monitor becomes a vital component of any karaoke system—performers often insist on the ability to hear themselves sing. Tapes of performances, distributed by emcees or recorded by performers on their home machines, are also used for self-monitoring. Performers review them, study them, sometimes even listen to them back-to-back with the original recordings.

Listening to tapes I've collected of my performances, I'm fascinated by the range of effects. My favorite is the Beach Boys' "Don't Worry Baby."

I've always identified with the oddball sentimentality of the group's *auteur*, Brian Wilson. I feel at ease with Wilson's placid original vocal and the campy lyrics that alternate between cosmic portentousness and drag racing. I'm less happy with my take on R.E.M.'s "Man on the Moon." Michael Stipe's original vocal is too moody, and the words too mystical for me to pull off. And I find my version of Prince's lover-as-roadster allegory "Little Red Corvette" all but unlistenable. My flat, nasally voice sounds out of whack with Prince's super-sexy lyrics, especially with Prince's own screeching, lowing, hyperkinetic vocal hanging over my head. Even my elocution is feeble. Where Prince says, "*A bod-deh like yawws oughtta be in jayyyl,*" I just say, "*A body like yours ought to be in jail.*" And it doesn't help when the emcee sees me off by announcing, "That was Prince as done by an accountant!"

Karaoke performance, then, is not blindly capricious and rarely involves the sort of free-floating identity play extolled by postmodernists. You try the part on for size and inspect its fit; you listen to yourself and imagine yourself from the audience's perspective. Still, if you like what you hear, you might briefly give yourself over to the song's persona. And if circumstances are right, you might realize new potentials within yourself, "burst[ing] forth from the bonds of narcissism by developing a sense of the other."[24]

Witness Greer, a regular at Spanky's, the college bar we visited earlier. She and her friends have already done recent hits by George Michael and the B-52's. Having run out of eighties tunes, Greer takes a chance on Janis Joplin's sixties vagabond anthem "Me and Bobby McGee." She starts off haltingly, halfheartedly, but as the song progresses she becomes absorbed by it. Soon, she's trembling and hollering the words, struggling to match Joplin's mercurial delivery. The normally impassive crowd at Spanky's applauds her effort.

The following week, four boys take the stage for the Joplin song and blithely desecrate it. They laugh, warble off-key, and quit after the second chorus. As if to rebut them and assert her own claim to the song, Greer requests it again. This time, she's into it from the start and doesn't miss a note. Later, she tells me that she hardly knew the song until she did it the previous week. "I know I don't look like Janis Joplin, but I really love that song." Her preppy appearance and Ivy League cachet seem antithetical to the song's reckless wanderlust—"*Freedom's just another word for nothin' left to lose*"—but in the course of two weeks she's found a space for herself in it.

Then there's Dan, an emcee I've befriended—a soft-spoken, middle-class guy in his early thirties. The most impetuous thing I've seen him do is excavate the chunks from the bottom of his coveted Ben & Jerry's ice cream. Having earned his M.B.A. just in time for the early-nineties recession, Dan views karaoke chiefly as a business venture. At shows, he operates the equipment and lets his wife Lori do most of the entertaining. When he does perform, he favors seventies, soft-rock numbers by the likes of Elton John, America, and John Denver.

One of the bars Dan and Lori work is Tinker's, an Irish pub in a working-class neighborhood of northeast Philly. Dan gets along well with the crowd there, even though his low-key performances, like his dress shirt and chinos, seem a bit out of place among locals howling hard rock numbers in t-shirts and jeans. Lori recalls one occasion, though, when Dan broke with form. "People knew Dan as Elton John and that type of music," she says, "and he got up once and did 'Paradise City,' by Guns N' Roses, and he did a really great job on it, and people freaked. 'I didn't know you could do that kind of stuff!'"

"Somebody had requested to do the song and asked me to help with it," adds Dan. "I had never sung it before, and I just started singing it and it was coming over the system. I was like 'God,' I really freaked myself out! I was like, 'Hey, this sounds pretty close, I'll keep doing it!'"

"Paradise City" is a favorite at Tinker's, an ecstatic rant that's worlds away from Dan's light-rock repertoire. It can be perilous for outsiders to perform a group's hallowed texts in this manner; their interpretations might be judged inadequate or false or demeaning. In Dan's case, though, "people freaked"; he looked into the mirror of the audience and saw his image reflected back approvingly. At the same time, he "freaked [him]self out," taking stock of his own performance ("It was coming over the system") and finding it worthy of Axl Rose's original ("This sounds pretty close"). Dan's "Paradise City" was, then, an exercise in self-transformation and self-discovery, exposing a hard edge beneath his soft, thirtysomething surface.

These karaoke role players display a capacity to realize desire, cultivate empathy, and enlarge identity through performance. In doing so, they afford further evidence that the very imitative, "twice-behaved" quality of performance can be its greatest source of power. As Ronald Pelias observes, "Saying the exact words of others in their unique form, in their complexity, in their style, in their intensity, helps performers to live in others, to share and understand worlds that are not their own. Such parroting functions as a procedure for coming, emotionally and intellectually, to know others."[25]

Dissident Voices

We've seen that karaoke performers, sensitive to direct social pressures and to the general milieu of the bar, tend to be cautious role players. Now and then, however, performers enact roles that are patently at odds with bar protocol. It is here that performers face their greatest challenge: not only to display and enact cultural values, but to question and perhaps even change them. At such moments, karaoke assumes a moral dimension, as performers' sense of commitment and crowd members' sense of tolerance are put to the test.

Such is the case at Shadybrook's, a bar nestled in the Pennsylvania Poconos, where quiet, conservative towns are intersected with bustling strips of resort hotels, and local folks cross paths with vacationers and itinerant workers. On karaoke night, the locals flock to Shadybrook's and mill around its spacious main room. Off to the side is another, smaller room where workers from the Highview, a nearby hotel, gather. They are younger and seem a bit incongruously cosmopolitan for this setting. Most are saving up or working their way through college; "passing through on the way to some other goal," as one puts it. The Highview boys are decked out in dress shirts and slacks, and the girls sport miniskirts, nylons, and heels. The locals wear t-shirts, flannel shirts, jeans, boots, and caps. The local women perform country songs by Patsy Cline, Tammy Wynette, and the Judds, and the men sing southern rockers by Creedence Clearwater and Lynyrd Skynyrd; the Highview people do smooth pop and disco numbers by Elton John, the Supremes, Gloria Gaynor, Bette Midler, and Air Supply.

A conspicuous presence among the Highview group is Wayne, who tends bar at the hotel and studies education and music at a nearby college. He's tall and heavy, with a boyish face framed by cropped, brown hair and a gold earring. His dress is loose and airy and all black: black, collarless, button-down shirt with sleeves rolled up to the elbows; black chinos rolled up to the shins; and shiny, black loafers with no socks. On the long ride from Philadelphia earlier this evening, my emcee friends, Lori and Dan, described the scene at Shadybrook's and advised me to watch for Wayne.

"He sings effeminate," Dan said.

"What do you mean?"

"He'll sing 'Over the Rainbow,' and 'If,' and all those pretty, slow songs," said Lori.

"I can hear people make little jokes," said Dan. "But when he's done, people clap."

"They do," Lori agreed, "because he's got a beautiful voice."

Already, Wayne's been tweaking the gender norms here and there. He's done duets with Highview girls on female vocals like Anne Murray's "You Needed Me" and Bette Midler's "The Rose." And when the hotel group did a collective rendition of Frank Sinatra's "New York, New York," Wayne joined the girls dancing Rockettes-style on the side rather than singing along with the men. (Meanwhile, a few local men in the audience carried on a mirthful yet slightly tense parody of the dancers.)

But his standout performance is a solo rendition of Tina Turner's "You'd Better Be Good to Me." The song opens with a pulsing rhythm, and Wayne, standing with his back to the crowd, shakes his hips and beats his fist in the air. Then he turns on his heel and sings in a breathy, sultry voice: *"A prisoner of your love, Entangled in your web."*

The song is a typical, mid-eighties dance number, a hi-tech, grandiose affair crowded with keyboard and percussion tracks. The persona disclosed by the lyrics is smitten, defenseless, delirious—a caricature that, to a great extent, has defined female pop vocals. All the while, it's hard not to imagine Tina Turner, miniskirted and shimmying in the shadow of Wayne's massive frame.

I've seen men do women's songs in karaoke bars before—men doing Patsy Cline's "Crazy" ludicrously off-key, doing Irene Cara's "Fame" in a piercing falsetto, doing Helen Reddy's "I Am Woman" in the voice of Arnold Schwarzenegger. Yet it is almost always played for laughs. Men rarely do female vocals without somehow "breaking frame,"[26] using overstatement and horseplay to slyly intimate, "This isn't really me." Female performers, on the other hand, readily do male vocals without resorting to such tricks. Outside of subcultures like the butch-lesbian performers celebrated by Judith Butler, masculine behavior is rarely reified and parodied the way that feminine behavior so often is.[27] Wayne, though, turns this equation around; he takes a text that's stereotypically feminine and renders it seriously. He not only performs femininity, but performs it unmarked and unexaggerated, with conviction and even reverence. He dances soulfully, shouts the words imploringly, sweating, red in the face. And, as Linda said, he has a beautiful voice.

And as Dan said, people make jokes. Jim, a beer-sodden local who's been regaling me with singing tips, refers to Wayne as "twinkle toes." "Watch his toes," Jim says, as Wayne now and then rises to the balls of his feet. Jim watches in silence for a while. "This guy sings very good," he says. "Some of the songs he sings are very quifty."

"Very what?"

"Quifty."

"What's that mean?"

"Like faggoty."

What's more surprising than Jim's apparent homophobia is his repeated admission that Wayne "sings good." Reactions to Wayne are riddled with "buts." Dan and Lori tell me he sings effeminately but beautifully, local men snicker through his performance but applaud when it's over. Many spectators seem caught up in his performance despite themselves. When this happens, Richard Bauman writes, "the performer gains a measure of prestige and control over the audience—prestige because of the demonstrated competence he has displayed, control because the determination of the flow of the interaction is in his hands."[28]

Wayne's performance can be taken as a sort of argument that it's okay for men to adopt women's voices, that women's voices can be as serious as men's, that men's voices can be as sensual as women's. Later, though, when I query him about his performance, he mentions none of this. And why should he? Little acts of bravery like his course through karaoke without elaboration. To the degree that karaoke performers "argue," they do so through enactments rather than exegeses, through emotional suggestion rather than logical explication. Like pop performance itself, karaoke is often at its most powerful "when its producers and consumers are least aware of any political or intellectual dimensions: when subversive constructions of race or sexuality suddenly confront the mainstream" in ways that command an immediate, visceral response.[29] The folks at Shadybrook's may laugh him off later, but for now Wayne's performance succeeds and possibly compels some in his audience to review their assumptions about gender and behavior, precisely because of the irrefutable pleasure that he and they take in it.

CHAPTER FOUR
RELATING IN THE LIMELIGHT

"N o-Talents making fools of themselves before complete strangers," ran an early description of karaoke singers in a national news magazine.[1] Here we come upon another common view of karaokists, one that pegs them as social misfits who lack meaningful relationships. As a sounding board for people's snap judgments about karaoke, I hear it often. What would possess people to do this? Is their self-esteem so low that they crave others' approval, or so high that they feel entitled to others' attention? Are their fantasy lives so grandiose, their real lives so impoverished? The consummate karaoke performer, in this view, is Jim Carrey in *The Cable Guy*, maniacally wailing "Somebody To Love" at the karaoke party that he's paid his guests to attend.

This image of karaoke performance as a form of sociopathy is a sign of how anxiety ridden public interaction seems to have become in U.S. society. Participation in public forms of recreation has declined for decades, as has membership in civic, religious, and school-based organizations. Social spaces such as bars, cafés, and town squares are hard to come by compared to times past.[2] Public life itself has come to seem exotic and threatening, the province of youth gangs and ne'er-do-wells. The forces behind this diminution of public life are myriad. Among the most often-cited culprits are the media; television is blamed for privatizing leisure time, the Internet for facilitating cyber relationships that render face-to-face interaction superfluous.[3] Certainly, our media habituation contributes to the sense of oddness surrounding public forms of interaction, including karaoke. A stock put-down of the more histrionic karaoke singers runs something like, "These guys think they're on TV," as if it were an act of insolence in any way to challenge the media's monopoly on public expression. Yet the responses to karaoke also point to larger anxieties surrounding relations in public in contemporary society. What sorts of relationships can we expect to form outside the spheres of family, friends, and coworkers? How do we reckon with the largely anonymous encounters of public space, which so often seem minimally involving and negligible, yet also seem to hint at something crucial about our society's quality of life?

Some have argued that our consecration of intimate relationships is itself a part of what alienates us from public life. Observers such as Richard Sennett, Malcolm Parks, and Eric Eisenberg discern a "tyranny of intimacy" in scholarly and popular discourse on relationships.[4] It holds that openness, honesty, and interdependence are unequivocal virtues in relationships, and that relationships are healthy and meaningful to the degree that they approximate the close ties of family and friends. Such an ideology has grave consequences for public life. On the one hand, public interaction is increasingly approached as a play of personality. We judge acquaintances and even strangers on the basis of their putative "character" rather than their performance of public roles. As Sennett writes, "we see society itself as 'meaningful' only by converting it into a grand psychic system." On the other hand, we increasingly see public interaction as "at best formal and dry, at worst phony," and we respond by seeking refuge within the sphere of close friends and family.[5]

An ideology of intimacy would seem fatal for an activity such as karaoke. Karaoke requires performers to take on a highly ritualized, circumscribed role in order to communicate with an audience that is likely to include more strangers than friends. Judged by standards of intimate communication, such an act seems pointless, and those who choose to perform it might seem shallow or vain. Indeed, some common designations of karaoke singers (i.e., extroverts, exhibitionists, fantasists) do transform it into something like a "grand psychic system," and obscure its potential social functions. And yet, karaoke continues to draw newcomers, many of whom have never before performed (let alone sung) publicly in their lives. They do so gingerly at first, and then a bit more confidently, and often, eventually, with utter commitment and finesse. Some of them find that karaoke can provide a way, not only to interface with strangers, but also to couch their close relationships in a public world and thus expand upon them. How do they manage it?

Below, I'll detail three ways karaoke performers respond to the challenge of relating in public. Some (especially novices) stay entrenched among familiars and regard karaoke with a mixture of curiosity and aloofness. Others straddle the divide between familiars and strangers, often by enacting their private relationships publicly. Still others (especially veterans) face strangers singly and try to muster some stable fellowship among them. This is not a series of stages that every performer goes through; as always, the process of communication is far too complex to be rendered by any such stage model. But they do seem to represent progressively mature and rewarding responses to the predicament of performance.

Night Tripping

On a sticky August evening, I sit alone in the basement pub of a college dorm outside Philadelphia, quiet except for some summer students and a factory-fresh singing machine. At the table in front of me, a half dozen pranksters celebrate their friend's birthday by gleefully interrogating him about which song he'd least like to sing. (Thus far the leading candidates seem to be Lesley Gore's "It's My Party" and the Angels' "My Boyfriend's Back.") Across the room, some girls who earlier put in a perky recital of Wham's "Wake Me Up Before You Go-Go" are debating what song to do next. Behind me sit three Deadheads who are here for no apparent reason. And in front of us all, taking up the bulk of stage time, is a twenty-strong mob of French, German, and Italian students in town for a month-long English program. In the home of the brave, these Old Worlders have seized upon karaoke, and they're in no hurry to relinquish it.

The Europeans wind their way through thirty years of American pop lore: Presley's "Jailhouse Rock"; the Beach Boys' "Surfin' U.S.A."; Sinatra's "New York, New York"; "Madonna's "Material Girl"; Michael Jackson's "Beat It." Each time the emcee calls out one of their selections, they trickle up a few at a time until their entire group is squeezed onto the tiny stage. The lyric monitor is off to one side of the stage, and they crowd around it in a semicircle so that we can't see their faces. Since they share only two microphones, most of them are inaudible; oblivious, they happily sing to one another. In fact, their performances are wholly directed toward one another. Despite the birthday crowd's shouts of encouragement, the Deadheads' smart-ass requests for "Dark Star" and "St. Stephen," and the emcees' desperate entreaties to "face the audience, please!"—they face one another, put their arms around

71

one another, dance with one another, laugh at one another. And when their songs come to an end, they applaud one another.

"I've learned as much English here as I have in my classes," one French guy tells me. They could hardly ask for a better primer than the musical lingua franca of American pop, with printed lyrics and visual narratives displayed in sync. This is the Europeans' third consecutive week here, and their studies are paying off. They not only deliver the lyrics flawlessly but add all the culturally correct flourishes—they mock-surf for the Beach Boys, they high kick in Rockettes fashion for Sinatra, they interject precision-timed screeches for Michael Jackson. Strangely, though, even as they pay tribute to American artists and play out fantasies of American extravagance, they do so in blissful isolation from the flesh-and-blood Americans who surround them.

Many people first encounter karaoke off the beaten track of their everyday lives, in those neither-here-nor-there places that have made so many American towns into "stopovers": hotels, motels, resorts, roadside inns, airport lounges. Some of the most riotous karaoke scenes I've witnessed are at places like the dingy after-hours bar a block off the boardwalk in the New Jersey resort town, or the motel lounge across the highway from the Florida theme park. An emcee who has worked several bars on the Jersey shore raves, "You get people from all over the country, and the attitude tends to be, 'Let's do it, man! Who cares? We came here to have fun!'" People perform with the abandon that comes from being certain that they will never see one another again. At the same time, there is a shallow, aloof feeling to these encounters that can't be dispelled. People stay to themselves or within their small groups, and interaction among strangers is limited to passing niceties.

These scenes bring to mind Daniel Boorstin's famous commentary on tourism. Boorstin contrasts the traveler of premodern times, who endured discomfort and danger in pursuit of novel experience, with the insulated, country-hopping tourist of modern society. The tourist's every move is calculated to guard against genuine contact with natives; they travel in packs, hole up in generic lodgings, and sightsee from the quietude of cars and buses. Their interaction with natives is limited to taking snapshots and haggling over souvenirs.[6]

Boorstin has been roundly, and rightly, critiqued. In characterizing tourism as insulated and prefabricated, he opposes it to an authentic mode of traveler–native interaction that is ill defined and elusive. His mass-culture elitism prevents him from seeing that thanks to tourism, millions have been able to visit places they otherwise couldn't have and thus expand their range of sympathies. Tourism need not be an escapist venture. Critics such as Mark Neumann and Erik Cohen have shown that even the most well-worn tourist sites can provide the backdrop for meaningful discovery of self and other.[7] Yet Boorstin's work retains its relevance as an account of one common disposition, not only toward travel but toward public leisure and public life. (Indeed, his work anticipated the more influential critiques of postmodernism and spectator culture.) Interaction in public is often approached from a touristic stance of detachment, as something remote and exotic, as if from behind glass.

Even at bars close to home, casual and novice karaoke performers often adopt this stance. Anyone who's tried karaoke knows, and anyone who hasn't tried it can imagine, what a challenge it can be at first. Life in the United States poorly prepares us for *any* sort of public performance, let alone public singing. The preferred coping strategy for karaoke neophytes is to take cover among intimates. They're the ones who perform in large groups and sing to one another more than to the audience. When they do sing solo, novices tend to restrict their gaze to friends offstage. Novice performances resemble "byplays"; they impose rules of private communication within public settings.[8] When it first appeared and when most everyone was new to karaoke, it came off like a collection of private parties that just happened to be taking place in the same room. And if you arrived alone—as not only ethnographers, but regular performers, sometimes do—you felt as though you were crashing all the parties.

Though tourists can be insular, they also can be all too candid, taking their exile as license to dispense with everyday manners and caricature their hosts' manners. So it is that, in Dennis O'Rourke's film "Cannibal Tours," Westerners abroad in New Guinea can throw a farewell party in which they paint their faces, joke about their souvenir penis sheaths, and lunge at one another in mock-cannibal fashion.[9] Likewise, karaoke neophytes and dabblers sometimes act in ways that make regular performers cringe. It is a novice who, after coyly taking the stage to humor his friends, can be found several beers later bellowing "Louie Louie" barebacked with his shirt tied around his head. It is a novice who shouts nonsense syllables and rubs his head against a speaker during the instrumental break of "Come Together."

As an audience member, I'm entertained by these performers, but I can't help feeling that they're doing these things in front of me, not because I mean so much to them, but because I don't mean much to them at all. Georg Simmel noted that in communication with strangers, we're liable to offer "the most surprising revelations and confidences, at times reminiscent of a confessional," precisely because we expect that they, or we, will move on—because we're not of one community.[10] The point is not lost on karaoke tourists, such as the woman who blithely tells me on her one and only visit to a Philadelphia karaoke bar, "It's easy singing in front of people you don't know." The expansiveness of some now-and-then performers seems rooted in the assumption that their relationship with their audience is a one-night stand.

Inherent in tourism, writes Edward Bruner, is "the binary opposition between us and them, between subject and object."[11] The touristic stance regards the natives as oddities, from a cool remove. One veteran performer recalls how he started. "My friends and I would go to these places, and sing, and make fools of ourselves, and laugh at all the people who took it seriously." I ask another guy who just performed for the first time, doing a garbled version of "Jailhouse Rock" with his buddy, how he thinks the audience liked it. "Overall, I think that they thought we sucked just like everybody else that gets up there," he says. "I get a kick out of the people that are serious when they sing, that think they're auditioning for *Star Search*. You know, you're in a friggin' bar." I tell him that some of these people probably do this every week, not only here but at other bars as well. "That's pretty weak," he snickers.

Sometimes this disdain for the natives breaks out into unabashed negligence. I once invited some students out to sing after their final exam so they could experience what I'd been raving about all term. My regular bar didn't have karaoke that night, so we ended up at a place that was new to us all—a little joint in north Tampa that shared a building with a liquor store and a fireworks outlet. We plopped down in the middle of the bar, taking up two large tables. Most of my students were karaoke virgins. They laughed nervously, certain that they'd bomb and almost eager to do so. They might have looked to the locals for guidance; instead, they flaunted their amateurishness and relied on one another's easy approval. Some women did a giggly version of "Girls Just Want to Have Fun"; one guy chose Nirvana's "Smells Like Teen Spirit," only he sang the words of

Frankie Valli's "Grease"; another took on a horrendous southern drawl for "The Whiskey Ain't Workin' Anymore." I got in on the act too, changing the tag line of the Everly Brothers' "All I Have to Do Is Dream" from "dream, dream, dream" to "cream, cream, cream," to get a cheap laugh from my students. One student brought a camcorder and circled us as if he were directing some crazed music video. Alternating with us, the locals did mostly devout, high-fidelity versions of country songs. We ignored them; when we weren't onstage, we talked among ourselves and nagged the emcee about when we'd be up again.

A few days later, the student with the camcorder sent me a copy of his video. I watched us hoot and holler and mug for the camera. In the background, I could catch faint echoes of the locals singing and glimpses of them impassively watching us sing. Who were these people? What could they have thought of us? We spent an entire evening with them, yet we hardly saw them. To us, they played the role of anonymous onlookers who were there for us to embarrass ourselves in front of. I had an urge to go back and apologize. We were like rock stars who breeze through town, terrorize the inhabitants, trash the hotel, and leave.[12]

Boorstin says modern tourism is imbued with "the comforting feeling of not really being there."[13] That night in Tampa, we were comfortable but we weren't really there. We evacuated our normal lives briefly but without entering into the lives of those we were visiting. For all our exhibitionism, we stayed very much to ourselves. Like all karaoke tourists, we came away with stories to tell, many of them collected on videotape like souvenirs. But we didn't come away with any sense of participation in a collective, public life.

Team Performance

Our group coped with the challenge of public communication that night by closing in on itself. But by the end of the evening, I noticed a change. Some students began critiquing their own and others' performances with an eye toward the larger crowd. "I gotta avoid those high notes," one young man said. "You should make more eye contact with the audience," a woman told her friend. They started to put more care into their performances. One group of women rehearsed a rudimentary series of steps and gestures for their take on the Supremes's "Baby

Love." Having been thrust into a situation of public performance for just a couple of hours, they began to take account of the strangers before whom they sang, and to help one another make a good show of it. They began to act more like a performing *team*.[14] In a team performance, individuals remain entrenched within their group, but the group becomes more outer directed, forming lines to open itself up to public life. Group members collaborate in appealing to the audience, synchronize their movements in relation to the audience, evaluate one another's conduct from the perspective of the audience.

Team performances are "complementary"; they often require different performers to play different roles.[15] Team members do little things to aid one another's performance, they feed each other lines and respond to each other's cues, rally and goad each other, correct or excuse or conceal each other's mistakes. Jennifer Mandelbaum's research on couples telling stories of their shared experiences reveals the subtle trade-offs of team performance. One partner might start with an allusion so vague that it's unclear what event she's thinking of or if she means to recount it. The other partner refers to the event head-on, and in the process does the first partner the service of forcing the story upon her. She picks up on his cue and thus ratifies him as a participant in the event and a co-teller of the story. As the story proceeds, they recount it from their differing points of view, acting out and reacting to one another's narrative halves in a fine-tuned game of show and tell.[16]

Similarly, as a friend of a prospective karaoke performer, there's much you can do to help her take the stage and optimize her encounter with the audience. It might do just to sit in the crowd and provide moral support, giving an occasional thumbs-up and mouthing, "You're doing great!" Or you might play the shill for her, cueing the audience's response by clapping and whistling and shouting, "This gal's good!" If you're not much of a singer, you can still offer the comfort of another warm body onstage. One woman would stand by her friend, hold her hand, and lip-sync: "I want to be there to support her but I don't want to throw her off." On the other hand, if your friend has more confidence in your singing than her own, you might hold a mike to back her up in case she strays off key, like a driving coach with a second steering wheel.

Sometimes your role may be to ceremoniously force your friend onstage, as when Sheila pulls Debbie up for a go at Madonna's "Crazy for

You." Sheila is an outgoing regular performer, Debbie a reticent first timer. Debbie slowly joins in and, lo and behold, she has a wonderful voice, so Sheila steps back and silently admires her friend. Debbie gestures for Sheila to join back in, but she refrains, and Debbie winds up singing solo. Afterward Debbie says, "I would have never went up there if it wasn't for her." And Sheila tells me, "To be honest with you, my whole role was to get her up there, because she's got a really good voice and I wanted her up there and she was too embarrassed to go up by herself. So I went up there and started off the song with her, then I kind of faded out."

The prospect of being forced to perform terrifies some karaoke neophytes. But there are those who don't want to sing and there are those who don't want to admit they want to, and a good teammate knows the difference. While the former do everything they can to deflect attention, the latter often draw attention to themselves with their expansive protests. As their friends prod them onstage, they laugh and blush and pull away, but not too insistently. It's a show that emcees and veteran performers find familiar, one that empowers people who may have yearned to sing publicly all their lives. What's impressive about such dramas is not just the subtlety with which teammates feel one another out, but the willingness of one teammate to take on the strong-arm role in the cause of enabling the other.

But to act as a team in karaoke means more than just making performance possible for one another or working out an expedient configuration of roles. Often performers communicate something *about* their relationships. Consider the middle-aged couple near the back of a Tampa bar. They sit alone, sipping whiskey and water, hardly talking or touching or even looking at one another. Then the emcee says, "Let's bring up Denny," and the man rises to the stage. "*Pretty woman, walkin' down the street*," he sings. He looks right at her, points at her, smiles at her. "*Pretty woman, say you'll stay with me.*" His voice turns pleading, his face is red. The crowd applauds. As he returns to the table, they embrace and kiss for a long moment. And then they sit, hardly talking or touching.

Karaoke performers do this sort of thing a lot. They home in on intimates in the audience, dedicate songs to them, stand over them or kneel before them, pull them onstage and sing duets with them. At first, it can seem trite. We're jaded from hearing songs passed around like valentines by way of wedding singers, lounge singers, and disc jockeys ("This song goes out to Jack from Jill"). But after watching a karaoke performer deliver a song on the verge of tears and fall into his lover's arms as he finishes, you realize what it can mean.

Often the last thing we're inclined to talk about with our intimates is the state of our relationships themselves. "Relationships are only rarely defined deliberately or with full awareness," Paul Watzlawick and his colleagues observe.[17] Men especially tend to take an if-it-ain't-broke approach to relationships, often regarding the very need for talk as a sign of relational problems. Instead of direct talk, we monitor our relationships through symbols and rituals, hints and innuendoes. Leslie Baxter and William Wilmot inventory the "secret tests" partners employ to gauge each other's commitment. One such test is public presentation. How do our partners enact our relationships before others, and how do they respond to our own enactments? Relationships, then, are publicly performed, and how they are performed can shape their destinies.[18]

To perform our relationships publicly carries risks.[19] On display, our relationships are no longer wholly our own. We run the risk of betraying secrets, violating expectations, discovering hidden discontents. Many of the songs under the "duets" heading on karaoke lists conjure romantic utopias that no real relationship can live up to; even a minor asynchrony between duet partners seems to clash with the rosy affinity projected in the lyrics. So it seems for the couple caught up in a syrupy version of "Endless Love." As a difficult line approaches, they both break off, look at each other and laugh awkwardly, like doubles tennis players when a ball passes between them.

Sometimes the asynchronies are more glaring, and performers find out things they might rather not have. At a crowded bar in Philadelphia's northwest suburbs, I sit with Marlene, a regular, and Cory, a newcomer. Having gone steady for three months with Cory, who's eleven years her junior, Marlene's decided to introduce him to the joy of karaoke. He won't go near the stage at first, so Marlene sings with friends and goes solo. She does Elvis's "Teddy Bear" with Guy, a middle-aged trucker, and "Suspicious Minds" on her own ("I always say that about Cory, he has a suspicious mind about me," she laughs). Finally, she coaxes Cory onstage for the Roberta Flack-Donny Hathaway number, "The Closer I Get to You." Cory seems completely devoted to Marlene. He looks straight at her and sings the tender lines with utter sincerity (although the track is a little high for him). Marlene seems more aloof, torn between Cory and the crowd. Is she concerned with impressing her friends? Embarrassed by Cory's singing?

Later, I ask them how they chose the song. "I like getting up there and just being myself and singing my favorite songs," says Marlene.

"Same with me," says Cory, "but with our relationship, we picked that song because it's special to us, to show the feelings we have for each other."

I ask how they felt about their performance. "I felt like I did good," says Marlene. "I pick songs that I can sing with my voice. I have an alto voice, and so I always sing those songs."

Cory looks at her a little sadly. "What about my voice?" he asks.

So it is that in performing our relationships, whether in karaoke bars or in everyday interaction, we tread a narrow path between our partners and our audiences. Our desire to let others in on what we share collides with our desire to seclude and safeguard it. Though we praise our glorious union to the skies, the song others hear from us may not be quite so harmonious as the one we have in mind. And yet, performing our relationships also allows us to reveal and validate them—as the line runs in so many pop songs, to tell the world about them. We perform our relationships to obtain recognition and support for them, to celebrate and enhance them, and, as Baxter says, out of "sheer joy and catharsis."[20] Like family photos or gift rings, ceremonial speeches or the acknowledgment sections of books, karaoke performances can work as testimonials to cherished bonds.

No less than language, gestures, and objects,[21] people in relationships cultivate a common reality through the music and other media they jointly canonize. Karaoke performers often choose songs to epitomize all that they share with their onstage or offstage partners. When a chest-thumping foursome of fraternity brothers takes the stage, they bust out with Sam the Sham's "Woolly Bully," the best frat-rock song this side of "Louie Louie." When a fellow in his twenties approaches the mike and dedicates a song to his grandmother in the audience, of course he does Barry Manilow—what better performer for a nice young man to dedicate to his grandmother?

Yet much of the relational communication in karaoke takes place outside the song's frame and conveys less pious devotion to the other than lighthearted camaraderie. "This is the worst song ever, and it's going out to Martin," announces Kate, whose friends Martin and James watch from the crowd, as she launches into Whitney Houston's "The Greatest Love of All." She sings, "*I believe that Martin is our future* [instead of '*the children are our future*'] . . . *show him all the fat he possesses inside* [instead of '*the beauty they possess inside*']." As she throws off cheeky references to her friends, she approaches one of them and hugs him; when he makes some smart-ass comment, she laughs, flips him the bird, and walks away. In close relationships, we often use such teasing insults not only to communicate our affection for one another but to perform it for others outside the relationship.[22] To loudly criticize your partner's song choice in mid-performance, to hand him your mike when he's hogging the limelight and leave him holding one in each hand, to conspicuously stick napkins in your ears—in the context of a serious duet, any of these moves would be traitorous to the team. But in the context of the casual rapport that many karaoke teams strive to project, they're just right.

It should be apparent that social relationships play so crucially into karaoke performance that people who never take the stage, and go unnoticed by the audience, are sometimes vital to the team. As a performer, you find that the mere presence of certain friends or lovers can enhance your performance. They're your foils, in relation to whom you fashion a persona to face the wider world; your consultants, who remind you of what you're best at; your witnesses, who guarantee that your peak moments will be remembered and recounted. And they, in turn, get a commensurate pleasure from witnessing the public display of a private persona they know so well. It reminds them of why they chose you as a friend or lover in the first place. In this strange situation, you suddenly seem very much yourself.

Branching Off

Relationships thus can give shape to performances, and performances can help make relationships intelligible to partners as well as outsiders. Yet performing in a way that does justice to your audience, and to your own feelings, sometimes means showing a self larger than even those closest to you can recognize. To adopt a certain voice, to sing a certain song, even to sing at all, may stretch the limits of intimates' images of you. In some measure, we all allow our loved ones to believe that the face we show them is our one true face, and we allow ourselves to believe the same of them.[23]

A popular icon like Madonna, insulated by the theatricality of stardom, can (in the documentary *Truth or Dare*) coolly feign masturbation onstage even as her father watches from the crowd. A karaoke performer, singing to a cluster of friends and strangers whom she will shortly rejoin, hasn't the same luxury.

To perform with any sense of independence from intimates or any sense of commitment to non-intimates often requires a sort of self-induced rite of passage, a separation, a pilgrimage. Explaining how certain individuals take karaoke to the next level, one emcee hits on a pivotal move. "You get a group of five or six guys going up. Then, you see, one of those five guys will branch off, and he'll get the book by himself. 'I'm gonna do one by myself.'" While it may be marked most clearly by the decision to perform alone, this "branching off" often involves much more. You find yourself taking seriously what was supposed to be a lark; instead of playing at doing karaoke, you find yourself just plain doing it. And if you start to incur nervous glances from friends, as overzealous hobbyists have incurred since Uncle Toby's military reenactments in *Tristram Shandy*, you may find yourself doing it alone.

Many regular performers have no choice but to attend by themselves. With each successive outing, it becomes harder to get any sort of quorum together. People who claim they're interested will back out at the last minute. People who go once or twice out of curiosity will cut their losses, driven off by the embarrassment of watching friends sing or the boredom of watching strangers sing or the fear of being asked to sing themselves. Close friends and lovers can be dragged along against their will but are liable to grow impatient. So, emcees are right when they claim that karaoke bars are good places to meet people; indeed, unless you like sitting alone, meeting people in karaoke bars may be less a luxury than a necessity.

One emcee observes, "About three weeks after you go into a place, you start seeing—I guess you'd call them the karaoke lovers. You start seeing this different clique that starts bonding together to do karaoke specifically." Often a particular performance or song provides the wellspring for a conversation or a relationship. A chemist in his thirties strikes up a friendship with a retired laborer when the older man buys him a drink to honor his take on Sinatra's "High Hopes." The chemist says, "When I got done singing, there wasn't a very big reaction to it. So he says to me, 'What are they all, idiots?'" A young Jewish man recounts how he once marched into a biker bar during the holiday season and did Adam Sandler's "The Hannukah Song." Though he'd had a couple of drinks and was "feeling pretty ballsy," he was sober enough to be a little nervous about flaunting an ethnic identity that was decidedly in the minority. Yet as he launched into the tune, "This whole table of people who looked like total rednecks started singing along with me. They knew the whole song by heart. Then they came over and talked to me, and it ended up that three of them were Jewish, and we got along great."

These contacts among regular performers are expedited by their focus. They are rarely very personal; performers relate to one another much in the manner of colleagues. Sara Cohen's account of interaction between amateur rock musicians in Liverpool could just as easily describe regular karaoke performers. "They joked and gossiped together; debated the merits of other bands; passed on contacts, advice, technical and musical skills, information about gigs [and] venues."[24] Performers may know one another only by their stage pseudonyms. Although their relationships may occasionally extend beyond the bar, more often they remain spatially and temporally bound.

Yet while performers' interaction is circumscribed, it is also civil and dependable and accessible. As Jane Jacobs writes of the street life of great cities, "most of it is ostensibly utterly trivial but the sum of it is not trivial at all." Like other sorts of non-intimate, civil communication, communication among regular performers provides "a feeling for the public identity of people, a web of public respect and trust."[25] Their contacts broaden horizons and promote tolerance, teaching them to cope with the heterogeneity of modern life. And their contacts are joyous. Performers' collective immersion in a skillful, artful activity can give rise to feelings of transcendence that may be rare even among close friends.[26]

As a regular performer, you become accustomed to relating to your audience, not as actual or potential acquaintances, but as a public—a group brought together by a common passion. Your performances become more generous, more sensitive to crowd and context. Instead of intimates, strangers serve as your anchor. You start observing people in the audience, guessing at what they might like, mapping out your appeal to them. You may even choose songs with particular spectators in mind: "Rock You Like a Hurricane" for the leatherette girls in front, "Mr. Blue" for the sixty-year-old couple in back. Or if you're really good, you might focus on no one—or everyone. Some experienced performers can consistently stand before a roomful of strangers and bring them half to tears. What's extraordinary is not just that they're capable of doing so, but that they have the will to do so for nothing in return but applause.

There's Michael, a gangly computer jock in his late twenties, who spends most of his Thursday and Saturday evenings at his two favorite Philadelphia bars, sometimes taking the stage five times a night. Though he's introduced some friends to karaoke, Michael is just as happy to arrive alone, since he's sure to run into other regulars. To hear him talk, in a quiet monotone with a slight stutter, you'd never take him for a performer; yet whatever he sings and whatever he sounds like, he gives it his all. If it's "Rocky Top," he'll borrow a cowboy hat off the head of a spectator and quickstep around the stage, hollering in a Tennessee drawl. If it's "You've Lost That Lovin' Feelin'," he'll pull some poor woman onstage and wail to her from down on one knee as though he couldn't live without her.

Michael understands each performance as a kind of mandate in which every member of his audience has an equal stake. "I'm not actually singing for myself, I'm singing for the crowd," he says. A good bar is one where the audience is willing to return the promise he offers them, where "people are into it, clapping, yelling, whistling. I hate going into a place where people just sit back and watch you." His pet peeve concerns the cliques whose members talk through most performances and only pay attention when one of their own takes the stage. "It's like you're at home, singing to your friends," he says. All regular performers share this craving to reach an audience beyond their friends at home, to conjure a group out of a roomful of strangers.

Eventually, though, performers hit a bump. The bar clientele finds its level, the dabblers disappear or become regulars, and you're left singing before much the same crowd week after week. At this point, it can *feel* like you're home among friends. When you're so comfortable onstage that you might as well be offstage, you face a new challenge—to rekindle the uncertainty that terrified and tantalized you at first. This is one reason why hard-core performers are constantly seeking out new venues. You become a traveling show, a barnstormer, and your home bar becomes the rehearsal space where you sharpen your act before taking it on the road.

Late in his career, Joe DiMaggio was asked why he continued to play so hard even when he was in pain from injuries and his team had already clinched the pennant. "There might be someone out there who's never seen me play before," he said.[27] Each new audience, maybe each new audience member, is an impetus for the actor to perform his script, the teacher to deliver her lecture, the comic to tell her joke one more time. Erving Goffman writes: "The teller's proper relation to his tale, his telling it as if this is the first time he has told it, is generated not by him, but by his having a first-time relation to his current listeners. The genuineness and spontaneity he can bring to his telling is generated by his current listeners' experiencing of genuine suspense; he borrows spontaneity from them. Effective performance requires first hearings, not first tellings."[28]

It might be added that performers borrow not only spontaneity but pleasure from their new audiences. Some outside observers find it pathetic that karaoke performers will trek long distances in pursuit of first hearings, and performers themselves sometimes are loath to admit it. Yet for many, it's what keeps them going.

Goffman suggests that new listeners "can appreciate that the speaker has told the same tale several times before" without it discrediting his performance.[29] Yet it seems that some experienced karaokists cannot resist giving the impression that they have a first-time relation not only to their listeners but also to their tales. "If a person is really good, and they know it," one emcee observes, "they'll go into a club where they've never done karaoke and no one knows them, and they'll get up there and act like they don't know what they're doing. They'll hold the mike funny, and they'll act like, 'Oh, help me, help me, I don't know if I can do this!' Then they come out with this great voice and everybody's like, 'Oh, my God!'" Beware, then. Some karaoke barnstormers are also hustlers. As they shyly take the stage and fumble with the equipment, they may be preparing to blow you away.

Gender and Power in the Limelight

Having considered how people negotiate relationships in the process of becoming regular performers, we face a lingering paradox. In order for karaoke to be sustainable, participants must to some degree bracket their personal ties and embrace their roles as performers and audience members. And yet much of karaoke's delight comes from the ambiguity of its roles—from the mystery of who participants are and where they stand as they face one another as performers and audience members.

Of course, even world-class performers with large, dispersed audiences cultivate some illusion of a more intimate mode of address (media theorists call this "para-social interaction").[30] Andrew Goodwin argues that, despite poor sound and oppressive crowding, people continue to brave large arena concerts out of a desire to commune with stars, to be in their presence and partake of their aura.[31] Anyone who's had front-section seats at a stadium concert knows what it's like when some megastar's eyes meet yours and you have the fleeting sense that he's singing directly to you; then his eyes drift away, and you shake off the thought and laugh at yourself. In a karaoke bar, though, where everyone is just in off the street, when a performer glances at you, it's not hard to convince yourself that he really *is* singing to you. And if you want, you can sing right back to him.

All this makes karaoke bars fertile fields for courtship. One emcee notes karaoke's potential as a come-on strategy for crafty Casanovas—one that is ambiguous and deniable, like small talk among dog walkers. "It allows a guy to walk up to a girl and talk to her without her thinking, 'What are you up to?' 'I'm not up to anything, I just like your dog.' Same with karaoke. A guy who doesn't know a girl can walk up to her and say, 'Hey, I'm really nervous about going up there, would you come up with me?' He can use it as an excuse to meet her."

True, a karaoke duet can be an excuse to meet someone, but it also can be much more than an excuse. For people who live their lives to the tunes of pop music, it can be a uniquely pop-musical way of romancing. As singing partners nominate tunes to perform, they can impress and appraise one another (Is he a Backstreet Boy or a Babyface?). As they settle on a selection, they can monitor each other's investment in their budding relationship (Is she willing to risk a love ballad or just an upbeat dance tune?). And as they perform, they can voice intensely personal sentiments under cover of song (Do you love me? Don't you want me? How do I get you alone?).

Yet this thrilling ambiguity of karaoke, this looseness of the theatrical frame that insulates it from real life,[32] also makes it a perilous courtship ritual. Even new relationships depend on some coordination of perspectives, of what you think of yourself and what I think of you, of what you think of me and what I think you think of me.[33] And karaoke, with its blurred boundaries, seems designed to cross up our perspectives at every turn.

I'm on the prowl for interviewees, and a swarthy, thirtyish woman sitting alone at the bar smiles at me. I recognize her as a performer and ask if we can talk karaoke; she gives me a whatever-you're-into shrug and says she'd be happy to. Debbie is from Hawaii, an army brat who's traveled all her life. She is self-possessed, friendly, maybe a little tipsy from the screwdriver she's been sipping. She responds to my questions with pleasant, meandering confessions of her love for singing and her loathing for her dull office job, her infatuation with Barry Manilow and the rapture she felt when she first saw him in concert. She notices my wedding ring and asks if my wife is with me. I say no, my wife detests karaoke. She tells me that I am a very nice person, and I tell her she is very nice, too.

Debbie goes up to do the Grass Roots's "Midnight Confessions," a sixties pop tune about secret desire. She sings intently, seldom looking up from the lyric monitor, though a couple of times she looks over at me and smiles. As the song closes, Debbie gets a warm ovation, yet she seems flustered when she returns to the bar. "I hope you didn't take that the wrong way," she says to me.

"Take what the wrong way?" I ask.

"That business about, 'the little gold ring . . .'"

I think for a second, and recall the lines from the bridge of "Midnight Confessions," lines I only half registered as Debbie sang them: *The little gold ring you wear on your hand, it makes me understand / There's another before me, you'll never be mine, I'm wastin' my time.*

I laugh. "Oh, no, I didn't think . . ."

"I realized I was looking at you when I sang that!" she chuckles.

"Oh, no!" We laugh together, both of us embarrassed.

"After I sang that line," she says, "I thought, 'God, what if his wife was here? What would she think?'"

"Really, don't worry about it," I say. "It hadn't even occurred to me."

We laugh some more, then talk some more. But the talk turns more guarded, and soon we are all business, closely following the interview regimen. Though Debbie picked out the Grass Roots song before we even met and sang it quite innocently, once she saw the potential connection between the song's ring and my ring, she felt obliged to ask whether I saw it. And once she asked, we both were left regretting the singing and the asking. Like some annoying matchmaker, the song seemed to intrude upon our faintly flirtatious conversation and leave us both guiltily proclaiming our innocence. This is the sort of trouble karaoke can get people into, or out of, when there is even a passing fancy between them.

Female performers have reason to be especially sensitive to the reception of their performances. Though it was more than a century ago that "public woman" was a synonym for prostitute, even in mid-1960s San Francisco, Sherri Cavan could observe that "the unescorted female [in a bar] is typically in a position where her virtue and character are indefensible."[34] Such antediluvian anxieties surrounding women's public appearance are palpable in karaoke. At a neighborhood bar in northeast Philly, a young man doing Guns N' Roses's "Welcome to the Jungle" can, without any apparent consequence, grab his crotch firmly as he screeches the line, "*Feel my . . . feel my . . . my ser–pen–teeeeeen!*" But when a woman at the same bar renders Patsy Cline's "Walking After Midnight" with even a hint of sexiness (smiling, eyebrows raised, swaying slowly), she is showered with catcalls. Some male emcees, otherwise vigilant in shielding singers from embarrassment, are not averse to introducing female performers with salacious wisecracks ("They're gonna strip for us, ladies and gentlemen!" "Who cares how she sings? Look at her body!"). And male audience members sometimes use women's performances as a pretext to accost them offstage or even join them onstage in mid-song.

The enviable vitality of Asian karaoke seems to hinge upon a segregation of the sexes that renders interaction between them moot. There are two karaokes in Japan. By night, businessmen gather at high-priced bars where the only women admitted are hostesses paid to coddle male patrons. By day, housewives, working women, and young people frequent "karaoke boxes," multiroom arcades where small groups rent rooms and machines by the hour for private use. Male bars are crowded, shadowy, brimming with drink and vice; female boxes are sheltered, brightly lit, alcohol free, and closely policed.[35]

American bars, of course, permit no such formal exclusion, yet patrons often seem to impose their own, predictable structure of privilege. At most bars I visit, male performers outnumber females, sometimes by two to one. Women who do sing, especially novices, are likely to be accompanied by male friends, and those who perform alone often call attention to male friends in the audience. The predominance of love-and-romance songs among female vocal numbers on karaoke lists (as in pop music generally) imposes a sort of double bind on female performers. Women who do such songs often make an effort to neutralize their romantic tension by laughing or tendering explanations like, "This song was chosen for me." In general, female performers tend to be more tied to intimates and less attentive to strangers in the audience—an unsurprising find, given women's marginalization from public life and relegation to "emotion work" in the larger culture.[36]

Yet if, as I've argued, relatively impersonal, collective activities like karaoke offer freedoms and pleasures not normally available within close relationships, then women have a particular stake in them. A woman who strives for the confidence and independence and benevolence of a top-notch performer finds it doubly challenging; a woman who manages to display these qualities with every performance appears doubly transformed. For instance, Carol, a regular performer at a bar in rural Pennsylvania, not only sings several times a night but serves as a volunteer facilitator on behalf of the emcees whom she's befriended. She coaxes patrons onstage, sings with them, and brings them together in novel combinations. Her husband, one of the few people she can't persuade to sing, sometimes comes in and watches with friends, yet she pays him and them no special attention.

Though Carol's manner is dynamic and engaging both onstage and offstage, she never allows herself to get too mixed up with anyone. On one occasion, she's working through Bobby Vinton's "Blue on Blue," and a short, chubby stranger named Angelo sidles up to her for an unsolicited duet. Carol seems a little disconcerted but stays on course, mostly ignoring the trespasser. Afterwards, the emcee politely asks Angelo if he'd like to put in a request himself. He declines, yet the moment Carol returns to the stage and starts into "You Don't Own Me," he's at her side again. This time, she gently tries to pull his mike away, but he holds on tight.

Angelo is a difficult lounge lizard to stave off, partly because he appears to be a karaoke newcomer who's oblivious to the boundary between performer and audience. Yet when he joins Carol a third time for "These Boots Are Made For Walkin'," she's had it. She summons Joanne, a friend who's about twice her age, and asks her to take over, claiming the song is out of her own range. After this, Angelo finally stops bugging Carol (though he does follow Joanne around for awhile, begging her to do "The

Impossible Dream" with him). Women who sing regularly thus may become not only more confident and outgoing, but more skilled at heading off the ordinary troubles that can result.

In her study of female rock musicians in England, Mavis Bayton notes the efficacy of the musician persona in women's encounters with rock's social world. Despite the notorious chauvinism of some male musicians and fans, women who establish their musical identities are regarded less often as sexual quarry, more often as workers, artists, and equals.[37] Karaoke, too, can allow women no less than men to engage more fully in public life.[38] Singing karaoke is about taking on a narrow role in the cause of doing things together. Like flying in coach, it can be confining, but it can also set you free.

CHAPTER FIVE
THE AUTHORITY SONG

ost of the people responsible for summoning karaoke shows into being claim to love their jobs. You can spend your evenings partying in bars with friends, be your own boss and make your own schedule, have breakfast after work and sleep all day. Many people first get into emceeing from a love of performing, lured by the prospect of singing at work and fiddling with a professional-quality karaoke system at home. Although the startup costs for a karaoke business are increasing as customers come to expect ever larger song selections, they're still modest compared to many other businesses.

Yet those who have only experienced karaoke as performers are often unprepared for some of the hassles of emceeing. Most emcees work independently and must act as their own promoters, technicians, and stagehands. They spend much of their time keeping books, traveling, and lugging around equipment. There's the aggravation of dealing with crowds who refuse to sing or individuals who refuse to stop singing, the stress of negotiating with stingy bar owners, the fatigue of spending four hours at a stretch on one's feet.

Most of all, there's the insecurity. Karaoke bars fall in and out of favor, and jobs are won and lost constantly. And because emceeing is relatively easy to break into, the field gets crowded and sometimes viciously competitive. You might do the hard work of establishing karaoke in a place and lose the job to some Johnny-come-lately who undersells you by a few dollars. You might cobble together enough two-hundred-dollar gigs to make a modest living, only to be squeezed out by moonlighters who happily will work for fifty dollars a night or hobbyists who will do it for free. Emcees often lash out at bar owners who award gigs to the lowest bidder, and at "undercutters," the untouchables of the karaoke business, who canvass the bars hawking second-rate services at cut-rate prices.

Yet while they bemoan the oversupply of services, emcees are hard pressed to articulate clear qualifications for their work. They often refer to themselves and the colleagues they most respect as "professionals," by which they only seem to mean that they get paid for what they do and do it well. Yet their use of the term may betray a certain anxiety that emceeing does not constitute a profession in any strict sense. There are no degrees, licenses, or unions for karaoke emcees. Some emcees are deejays or musicians who see karaoke as a way to put their amps to use on off nights; others are dabblers who, after piecing together a decent home system and hosting a party or two, figure they might turn a profit from it. Most emcees get their first gigs through personal contacts and are trained on the job. Established emcees often grouse about performers who think they can emcee, yet many of them hire performers as assistants or stand-ins for bathroom breaks or vacations. Regular customers are, after all, the readiest source of labor for emcees who want to expand their operations or who need extra help.

When emcees pitch their services in newspapers and flyers and web pages, they highlight the technical features of their shows: their song selections, their state-of-the-art equipment, their prowess at the controls. These things certainly matter, and when they go to extremes they can make or break a show. (I know of emcees who carry thirty thousand titles or more; I know of others who carry a couple of photocopied pages worth of titles.) Yet when performers (and emcees themselves, in their reflective moments) are asked what defines a great emcee, they're more likely to emphasize social skills. "The biggest thing is that you have to be friendly and outgoing," says Tony Shaw, who employs a stable of karaoke hosts in the Philadelphia area. "To be a good emcee, you have to be able to get along well with people." People attend karaoke bars not just to sing but for a certain sort of experience, and central to this experience is the quality of their interaction with the emcee and the emcee's personal treatment of them as performers. A good emcee reads and responds to her performers with such sensitivity that they come to see her as an ally in their individual struggles with karaoke.

Emcees' crucial assets, then, are not traditionally masculine, technical skills, but traditionally feminine, "people skills." They must excel at listening and supporting, mediating conflicts and managing crises. It's no surprise that many emcees are women, or that, when emcees work in male-female pairs (as many do), it is the women who usually work the crowd while the men work the equipment. In its demand for putatively feminine, interpersonal competencies, emceeing resembles many other jobs broadly categorized as service professions. Like flight attendants or fast-food servers, bank tellers or beauticians, emcees are in the business of "emotional labor," summoning positive feelings within themselves in order to induce positive feelings in others.[1] And for emcees, as for other service workers, these displays of affect are dictated not by personal intimacy or social custom, but by their very livelihood.

Yet emceeing differs from other service professions in significant ways. Employees within many such professions find their emotional labor engineered from the top by owners and managers. Through training and surveillance worthy of a militia, workers at Delta and Disney and Amway and Mary Kay are imbued with unremitting courtesy and enthusiasm.[2] By comparison to such service-industry megaliths, the karaoke business gives workers much more freedom from direct supervision. Emcees are mindful of the expectations of bar owners and, among those who work for larger outfits, bosses. But by far, they are most beholden to customers. "Your key measure of success is the development of a cadre of loyal regulars," states one manual for emcees.[3] Some singers will follow a favorite emcee from one gig to another like groupies, providing a clientele that she can sell to new bars. Emcees rely on customer allegiance for a modicum of job security and leverage against fickle owners and undercutters. As this implies, the emotional demands of emceeing are no less severe for being imposed from below rather than above. To win their loyalty, emcees often feel compelled to spoil customers with drop-of-a-hat displays of empathy, nurturance, and deference.

Moreover, emcees bear responsibility not only for pleasing individual patrons but for "routinizing" the overall event. They're expected to draw a steady flow of volunteers, look after the rotation, get people onstage and offstage expeditiously, police onstage behavior, and fill dead air between performances. Robin Leidner contends that all service workers face the challenge of enforcing work routines,[4] but for emcees this challenge is exceptional. They work alone or, at best, in pairs. Often, they work with novice performers for whom karaoke's rituals remain somewhat strange.

And always, they work in "found spaces," bars and clubs with preexisting codes of behavior. Like street performance or experimental theater, karaoke takes root in the world, blurring the boundary between art and life.[5] A stage is jury-rigged in a corner of the bar, the drinkers are handed microphones, a switch is thrown, and suddenly it seems like anything can happen. But emcees don't want *anything* to happen. They're not out to provoke or edify, but to make customers happy, make things go smoothly, make a buck. No less than other service workers, emcees must standardize the behavior of customers, but in an environment where customers' behavior tends to be anything but standard.

Routinizing Karaoke

"Anyone here not know how to do this?" Once an emcee has spent a few weeks in a locale, once she's established the drill and primed the crowd, that's all she might need to say to get things going. The regulars start submitting songs as she walks in the door, they march onstage the moment she calls on them, they sing with poise and self-control. But when the same emcee hauls her gadgetry into a new bar, she's likely to be greeted with blank stares. Many customers might never have experienced karaoke and might not even know what it is. And they might not be particularly ingratiating; many may feel they're doing just fine with their beer and their idle talk and their jukebox. Even owners are sometimes skeptical, and only let emcees set up shop on a "free trial" basis until they prove they can draw a crowd. Like early devotees of *The Rocky Horror Picture Show*, who were routinely ejected from theaters for shouting and throwing rice until theater owners started seeing their profit potential, emcees often come off as noisy apostles of some cultic observance.[6]

Thus, smart emcees assume little knowledge or interest when they take on a new job. Rick and Sara Gandy, a successful father–daughter team, recently started a gig at a south Jersey nightspot called Spender's. Sara is a bubbly, genial host who's acquired a knack for rearing jaded old drinkers into avid karaokists. In her opening speech, she takes nothing for granted, bringing the crowd along like toddlers taking their first steps. She explains how the machinery works. "Now these songs I have up here on laser discs, they have the background vocals and the background music. But they don't have the lead voice, and that, ladies and gentlemen, is where you come in." She gives potential singers a sense of control by clearly relating the procedure. "What I want you to do is look through the books, pick out a song, fill out a request form, and bring it up to me. I'll call you up on the mike . . . All you have to do is sing the words as they change color." She plays on the secret desire to sing that, she knows, many of them harbor. "You can't tell me that with thousands of songs to choose from, there's not one in there that you haven't sung, fixing your hair or driving your car." And she assures them that their reception will be positive. "When you're done, everybody's gonna clap real loud."

At this stage, routinizing karaoke is chiefly a matter of attracting performers—and attracting performers is chiefly a matter of salesmanship. Like any good seller, an emcee must begin by identifying prospects. Less experienced emcees tend to take a hit-or-miss approach; some seem to subscribe to the timeworn, direct-sales credo that with enough effort, anyone can be persuaded to buy anything. I know one such emcee, Nick Healy—actually a bar owner who's acquired a karaoke machine and, like certain professional sports team owners, has convinced himself that he's best fit to run it. Each week, Nick blunders through his ad-lib opening spiel, and if he doesn't attract any singers, as he often doesn't, he blunders through it again. Now and then, though, he gets desperate and futilely begs some random member of the crowd to perform. On one occasion, Nick blindsides two college-age women in the middle of a conversation. "How about a song from you two?" he says.

At first they blow him off, but when he persists, they leaf through the song menu, whispering and giggling. One of them, a sandy-blond-haired woman with a crooked smile, looks up and says to Nick, "If you do 'Billie Jean,' then we'll do one."

Laughter ripples through the crowd, and people start chanting, "Billie Jean! Billie Jean!" Soon enough, we're all treated to Nick's garbled version of Michael Jackson's dance-funk classic. As the song ends to raucous applause, Nick says to the two women, "Now it's your turn."

The woman with the crooked smile looks up again. "If you do 'Girls Just Wanna Have Fun' . . ."

Nick finally gives up on them, sadder and wiser—like the real estate broker in the play *Glengarry Glen Ross* who hawks some swampland to a couple of pensioners only to learn that their checks are bad and they just like talking to salesmen. Emcees who don't bother to get a feel for their customers are asking for this kind of trouble. They waste their time on non-prospects and end up empty-handed or captured by their game. Any good salesperson, from the corporate account exec to the carnival barker, learns to identify customers' needs and assess their commitments.[7] Shrewd emcees sometimes can be found sitting at the bar an hour before show time, surveying patrons' general levels of performance pluck as well as their specific musical tastes. People who initially refuse to sing will get that kid-in-a-candy-store look when the emcee lets slip that she just got hold of a disc with the new Fatboy Slim hit or the old Gene Autry gem.

A seasoned host will open the show by doing one or two songs on her own, strategically chosen to pique the crowd's interest. And as she sings, she eyes her quarry. There are the ones who ignore her and try their best to talk or play Ms. Pacman or do whatever it is they do. There are the ones who throw a bemused glance her way every so often to see if anything interesting is happening. And then there are the ones who watch her rather intently, perhaps vaguely singing along with her, perhaps even prying open a song menu and gleaning the titles. "You can actually look out at the crowd and pick out who's gonna sing, who might sing, and who's definitely not gonna sing, and you just work the ones who you think are gonna sing," says one emcee. Once an emcee senses who wants what she's got, she doesn't need to twist arms; she only needs to beckon.

The beckoning has to be tactful, though. Emcees know that accosting customers too bluntly or aggressively can backfire. As one says, "You never tell them, 'I'm gonna get you up here, I'm gonna make you sing.' People will leave if they think they're going to be approached directly." Yet many customers won't sing *without* being solicited in some fashion. Many would like to appear, and maybe to feel, as though they're answering a higher call than that of their own inner peacock. They need some justificatory plea that they can nobly give in to.

So emcees have to furnish incentives—or excuses disguised as incentives. Sometimes, at new gigs, they'll give away t-shirts or pitchers of beer. "Then it's like, 'I'm not coming up here because I want to be here, I was given something free to get up here,'" jokes one host. Apart from freebies, though, emcees learn to offer subtler rewards: the satisfaction of giving, the security of belonging. Consider Steve Raymond, who runs an early evening show in the adjoining bar of a franchise restaurant outside Philly. He often faces crowds of cranky, hungry people waiting for tables. To spark the show, he scopes out the ones moving their lips or scanning the song lists. "I walk over and say, 'Listen, you've got to help me out, it's going really slow tonight. If people don't start coming up there, I'm gonna lose my job, and I need it.'" By requesting certain crowd members' assistance, Steve positions them as deputies or shills in the staging of his show.[8] Though he's only twenty-one and single, Steve seems to have picked up on an old parenting trick—keep the older kid in line by planting it in his head that he's helping with the baby.

If customers have even a touch of karaoke fever, though, an emcee shouldn't have to resort to anything so explicit to enlist their aid; it's enough just to treat them warmly. One way service workers both accomplish and conceal routinization is by modulating their stock interactions with personal touches.[9] Disney World workers are trained to scan park visitors' outerwear for their first names, Marriott bellhops to notice and comment on the home cities of hotel guests.[10] A good emcee circulates around the bar and greets past and prospective performers. He sits with them awhile and learns a bit about them, works up nicknames and tosses off inside jokes. (Another advantage to emceeing in pairs is that one partner can see to the stage show while the other works the floor.) He makes all his customers feel like they have an inside connection, and before long they're lining up to appoint themselves his weekly, unpaid assistants. At one bar, the night's first singer opens by declaring, "I'm always bailing Charlie [the emcee] out." At another bar, a college kid who, with three friends, has just treated an indifferent crowd to "Play That Funky Music" tells me he feels responsible to "keep [the emcee] going."

"What do you mean?" I ask.

"He's up there saying, 'Okay, I need someone to come up here and sing,' so we'll sing a couple of songs to get people in the mood," he says. "I've come nights when no one wanted to sing, and I had to sing like eight or nine songs with my buddies."

Whether by design or not, then, emcees' wholesale hospitality helps them generate the flow of volunteers they need to make karaoke happen. But there's a catch. Treat people as colleagues or as kin, and they're liable to expect all the benefits of collegiality or kinship. All service workers face customers who clamor for the truly distinctive, personal ministrations that service organizations so often advertise. Karaoke performers who have been led to think of themselves as emcees' little helpers have a habit of calling in their debts now and then with requests for special treatment. Sometimes, these requests are merely self-seeking—to skirt the rotation, or sing two or three songs in a row. Other times, they're quite understandable, given the uncertainties of performance—to sample a song before singing it, or restart a song in a different key, or change songs at the last minute. In any case, emcees who indulge customers' special requests risk unsettling the routine. "Customers who do not behave as expected have the same effect on service organizations that ill-fitting parts or unusual specifications have on assembly lines."[11]

Minding individuals while also minding the show becomes especially tricky at that pivotal moment in the life of every good karaoke gig when the thing suddenly "takes." At some point, customers shed the trappings of modesty and begin scrambling up to the stage with the sort of infectiousness that social scientists put down to "crowd behavior." Having begun by begging for volunteers, the emcee may find herself with a two-hour rotation of thirty or more singers. Now stage time is at a premium, and people will go to absurd lengths to expedite their turns at the mike. "It reminds me of babysitting," says one emcee. "You get there and the kids are all quiet, they hide in the corner, and you coax them out, and then they're little monsters." Emcees see it all, customers who submit songs under multiple names in the hope of multiplying their stage time, who cajole their friends into submitting so they can stand in for duets, and who coolly reach for their wallets and pull out a twenty- or fifty-dollar bill (most hosts don't take bribes; some do). Mostly, though, customers simply sidle up to the emcee and start laying on the pretty pleases. Emcees are thus overwhelmed with calls for favors just when they're most vulnerable to accusations of favoritism. At such times, they may find that the rapport they've worked so hard to cultivate has come back to haunt them.

Emcees Who Love Too Much

I've considered how emcees project warmth and gratitude and approachability in order to soft sell customers on the idea of singing. But service workers don't just use emotions to sell products; often their emotions *are* the product, or part of it.[12] Airlines sell friendly service as well as plane rides, and theme parks sell upbeat, "magical" service as well as coaster rides.[13] Emcees, too, sell a particular sort of service. People go to karaoke bars not just to sing with the aid of sophisticated equipment, but to be lavishly introduced, applauded, and praised, and emcees are typically eager to oblige.

Indeed, many hosts are notorious for the over-the-top enthusiasm with which they seem to greet each and every singer. Audiences are relentlessly prodded and pestered into applauding. "What I like to do," one emcee tells me, "is say, 'Everybody clap one time real loud for me, so I can get an estimate of about how loud you guys can be.' Then if I notice that somebody's not getting applause . . . I just say, 'All right, put your hands together! These girls really worked up a sweat up here!'" Most hosts come down hard on audience members who have the gall to heckle performers. The lucky ones are simply ejected. Some emcees borrow the stand-up comic's trick of turning the tables and heckling the heckler ("Thanks for your opinion, sir, but opinions are like hemorrhoids because sooner or later, every asshole gets one!"). I've heard of one emcee who forces hecklers onstage to sing "I Touch Myself," the Divinyls's paean to onanism.

It's easy to dismiss emcees' cheerleading as specious protocol, like the simulated ardor of sex workers. Yet in most cases, emcees' shows of support seem sincerely felt and connected to larger work values. Emcees are nearly unanimous in their agreement that all karaoke performers have something of value to offer and that every performer deserves attention and recognition. I could cite dozens of statements by emcees to this effect: "This is not for professionals, it's just for everyday people"; "It doesn't matter how good or bad you are, there's always someone better or worse"; "The karaoke attitude is strictly one of positive support"; and so on. When emcees talk about this, they don't seem like they're selling a line in order to further their careers. On the contrary, they seem like they've adopted a belief as a result of their careers. It's an occupational attitude that people find waiting for them when they become emcees.

And yet, unconditional support is easier to promise than it is to deliver. For one thing, audience members often feel put upon by all the boosterism. Most people attend karaoke bars not just to sing but to listen, and some attend only to listen. Notwithstanding the current fanfare about interactivity, some folks enjoy being an audience.[14] While they may understand that karaoke is "not for professionals," many listeners would like to hold performers to certain standards. Sometimes they shower singers with applause and requests for encores, other times they casually tune singers out, and other times they converge upon the emcee in tears, whispering, "Please don't let that guy back up there." There have been documented cases of customers leaving bars en masse to escape the vocal onslaught of particular performers.

By encouraging applause for performers who don't necessarily deserve it, emcees ask audiences to carry on a sort of collective deception. They also run a risk that the performers themselves will take the deception to heart. "There's a woman who used to come in," says one emcee. "She got all dressed up, I mean to the nines. Got up there and performed like she was Madonna, and the God's honest truth was she wasn't that good, but she thought she was. So I had to treat her as if she was star-quality." Such singers are an imposition upon the emcee; they seem to take advantage of her generosity. The emcee's dilemma here is comparable to that of the Santa Claus who must remain jolly even when toddlers pee in their laps, or the Disney character who must endure blistering heat and blackouts rather than remove his costume head and dash some child's fantasies.[15] By suffering such singers gladly, emcees and audience members become "enablers" of their prima-donna pretensions.

Emcees' indiscriminate encouragement of performers is not just an imposition on the audience; it can also leave some performers feeling cheated. Singers who are gifted (or who think they're gifted) sometimes hanker for a more meritocratic dispensation of accolades. A nagging dissatisfaction creeps over them, best expressed perhaps by the W. S. Gilbert line from *The Gondoliers*, "When everyone is somebody, then no one's anybody." To dispel comparisons between performers, some emcees even go in for a kind of reverse discrimination, making excuses or casting teasing insults at their more skilled singers. "Those guys are part of a theater troupe, so don't be intimidated by them, they do this all the time," explains one emcee after an exceptional group performance, joking that the group won't be allowed to sing anymore because they're too good. Emcees' responses to performers sometimes resemble American parents' responses to their children's art, where every little scribble goes up on the refrigerator door. The risk here is that performers will pick up the same message Larry Gross says children pick up: that their appraisers don't actually know or care much about their efforts.[16]

More subtle still is the influence of this endless support on the emcee's own sense of self. Emcees sometimes seem to bend over backward to maintain their own conviction of every performer's right to be heard and applauded. For reasons of self-presentation or occupational ideology or simply getting along, some emcees become "deep actors," throwing themselves into their supporting roles as unreservedly as any Actor's Studio veteran: "By taking over the levers of feeling production, by pretending deeply, [the worker] alters herself."[17] Arlie Hochschild gives the example of a flight attendant describing how she deals with "irates," or problem customers: "I pretend something traumatic has happened in their lives. Once I had an irate that was complaining about me, cursing at me, threatening to get my name and report me to the company. I later found out his son had just died. Now when I meet an irate I think of that man."[18] This worker copes with customers' anger by mustering sympathy for them, yet it's hard not to feel sympathy for the worker herself, who can only stay her own anger by dreaming up worst-case scenarios of her customers' states of mind. In the process, she not only excuses her customers' rudeness but reprimands herself for any welling of resentment toward them, saying to herself, in effect, "I must not think that."

Emcees, too, learn to use their imaginations to manufacture sympathy toward performers. "The woman was tone deaf, horrible," one emcee jokes about a performer. "It was like, 'Oh my God, the cats are fighting.'" Yet almost immediately, the emcee's voice becomes serious and she checks herself. "I don't care what people thought. She wasn't good, but this experience meant something to her. Maybe the song meant something to her. She had her chance to get up there and be Whitney Houston for five minutes. . . . You have to make people comfortable and make them feel good about it, regardless of how they performed." Similarly, when one emcee opens an Internet discussion with the mildly caustic query, "Do all the worst singers want to sing all the hardest songs?" he is flooded with negative responses. "Did you ever once think," another emcee shoots back, "that maybe that guy who did the off-key rendition of 'Unchained Melody' was thinking of the first time he met his wife? Did you ever think that maybe the lady who Roseanne Barred herself through 'You Make Me Feel Like a Natural Woman' was trying to send a message to her husband?"[19]

Even in backstage discussions, these emcees rouse themselves and one another not just to express but to feel unqualified benevolence toward customers. And in their struggle to find something worth celebrating in every performance, they fall into a routine of deep acting, "chang[ing] images, ideas, or thoughts in the service of changing the feelings associated with them."[20] They spin stories of their customers' fantasies of stardom or communions with loved ones or struggles with stage fright, and they lay the burden of providing happy endings for these stories squarely on themselves. No wonder that, like others whose work involves deep acting, emcees sometimes complain of "burnout." Some risk losing their sense of emotional groundedness even off the job. They find themselves walking around with vacant smiles on their faces or instinctively applauding for songs playing on their car radios. Others suffer alienation from the emotions expected of them on the job. They find it is all they can do to plaster on smiles and offer token applause as yet another unexceptional singer concludes yet another take on "The Rose" or "The Greatest Love of All."

Gentle Dissuasion

While the support demands of their work can make their mark on emcees' psyches, these effects need to be put in context. The theorizing around emotions and work too often frames the issue in black-and-white terms— people bring authentic, private feelings into the public world of work where they're transmuted and commercialized.[21] Such a perspective leaves the worker few choices. She can become a deep actor who immerses herself in her role, or a "surface actor" who mentally disengages herself from it. In the first case she risks burnout, in the second case, cynicism.[22] Yet in work performances, as in many everyday performances, most of us teeter delicately between cynicism and sincerity.[23] Many service workers understand their work as involving acting but don't experience it cynically. Though emcees claim to support all performers equally, in practice, they find ways of screening and framing performances that involve surface as well as deep acting. Effective emcees are mobile and shifting in their alliances with performers and audiences, and at times they find it expedient to gently prod or discourage or deceive performers.

This process is set in motion before the performer takes the stage, the moment that he approaches the emcee to request a song. The first few such encounters between performer and host are likely to involve nothing more than brief pleasantries, but after a few songs or a few weeks worth of songs, they begin to take the shape of semiprivate consultations. The emcee's role in such encounters becomes comparable to those of other workers who deal with highly valued, ego-laden features of customers' physical presence, such as clothing store clerks or hairstylists.[24] For customers mulling over song menus or haggling over hairstyles or assaying new clothing ensembles, these workers act as surrogate audience members, responding to customers' choices as the latter rehearse situations to come. And in all these contexts, "a particular sort of intimacy may develop between the two parties to [the] transaction."[25] Even when there is no one else waiting to sing, and it would be unnecessary from a practical standpoint, performers often choose to write their song choices out, hand them to the emcee, and have them acknowledged and confirmed.

In the boutique and the salon, these semi-intimate encounters "center around the customer's body";[26] in the karaoke bar, they center on the voice, a comparable source of vanity and shame. Like other "minor stigmas"—thin hair or a thick waist—the performer's vocal imperfections become objects of inquiry and therapy.[27] As performers come to trust them, emcees offer tactful advice on general technique ("hold the mike lower" or "drink water and lemon to clear your throat") as well as specific decisions about text and persona. For my own performances, I often choose female vocals—partly because some of my favorite songs are female vocals, but also in order to gauge reactions. Emcees sometimes greet these requests with gentle provisos such as "That's a little high for you" or "Isn't that a woman's song?" They seem to have one eye toward my satisfaction, another toward the expectations of the audience and the tenor of the show. They advise and protect me, and at the same time they keep me in line.

In these consultations, emcees lay claim to an expertise that can become central to their occupational identity. Many emcees make an effort to familiarize themselves with the songs in their repertoires so they can answer questions and make suggestions. "Learn your music, country, rock, standards, classics," writes one contributor to an emcees' Internet list. "You should be more knowledgeable about your music than the average person, that is why we get paid to do this job." Another contributor intimates that part of what keeps him going as an emcee is "thinking and hoping that the next singer will have made some improvement . . . or that they have listened to your thought on them singing a different song and enjoyed the change."[28] By counseling customers, emcees and other service workers mark their turf, making a bid for authority and status that complicates their role as emotional supporters. In her study of a suburban New York hair salon, Debra Gimlin notes how beauticians use their professional expertise to offset status differences with their upper-middle-class clients. They regale customers with wisdom on recent styling trends and their aptness to customers' particular features, just as emcees take stock of new songs and their aptness to performers' voices.[29]

Yet workers' bids for expert status are not always successful. Rather than creative consultants, they're sometimes treated as mere technicians whose job is to cheerfully carry out customers' wishes. The beautician's yuppie clients ignore her advice and opt for the same ho-hum hairstyles they've always worn; the emcee's customers view him as the grunt who works the controls, and sing whatever they please. At such times, workers must hold their tongues as customers walk off with the wrong haircuts or the wrong songs. (One thinks also of the Italian chef in Stanley Tucci's film *Big Night* who can barely contain his horror when a gastronomically naive customer demands a side of spaghetti with her risotto.) Gimlin concludes that beauticians are "more like service workers than professionals" because they are "financially and emotionally required to defer to their clients' judgments."[30] Yet in fact, many kinds of service workers must strike a careful and ever-shifting balance between expressing professional advice and providing emotional support.

When a performer disregards the host's plea to try a different song (or maybe try resting his voice a while), less equivocal measures may be called for. The emcee, after all, controls access to the stage. More than a consultant, she can be a gatekeeper or censor. Emcees recognize that their work involves a degree of puppet mastery over performers and audiences. Like club deejays or radio programmers, they regulate the emotional rhythms of bar crowds through their choices. "We're in charge of reading the crowd," says one emcee. "When we control who's gonna get up, in essence we're controlling how the crowd's gonna react." Though most emcees insist that they call on performers in the order of their submissions, some are not above tampering with the rotation to admit variations in tempo and genre; to space out overdone or already-done songs; and, most problematically, to deep-six singers who are unruly or uninspired or simply unlistenable. When asked how he deals with his less popular singers, Philadelphia emcee Jerry Pellini confesses, "Sometimes I remember their name, and if that slip keeps coming up, I'll just keep putting them at the bottom. Just for their own good, y'know?"

By burying or discarding slips, emcees call upon another set of tactics available to workers ostensibly in the business of service—that of delay, mystification, and selective oversight. Emcees are sheepish about this business and rarely discuss it, least of all with the expectant souls whose turns onstage are quietly elided. Yet it isn't—it can't be—exactly a secret. Performers often privately and obsessively monitor the status of their submissions, emcees know they do so, and performers know that emcees know. Emcees don't count on performers overlooking their exclusion; on the contrary, they count on them noticing it and getting the message. "They put their slips in and they're not being called," says Jerry. "Believe me, I think they know."

One of the bars Jerry works is J. R. Mitchell's, a bustling venue in Philly's northwest suburbs. At Mitchell's, Jerry often accumulates a half-inch-thick stack of submissions before he even opens the show, and every other performer seems to be a current or former band member. On my first visit here, I notice a man peering over my shoulder at my field notes. "What're you writing?" he asks. I explain my opus and we start talking. Guy is a truck driver with long, grayish hair, a beard that's due for a trim, and a half-drunken, half-crazed look. Jerry refers to him as Charles Manson, though he looks more like Dennis Hopper. Since Guy is the first person in the bar to acknowledge my presence (he later admits that he mistook me for either a talent agent or a government agent), I hang with him. I soon realize that as an ethnographer, ever marginal, I only make things worse by joining ranks with other marginal men. And here, it will cost me not only as an ethnographer, but as a singer.

Jerry lets Guy loose onstage once, early in the evening when it's not too crowded, and he offers up an atonal version of Zagar and Evans's "In the Year 2525." Later, around his fifth Jim Beam and soda, Guy convinces me to pitch in for a duet on Aerosmith's "Dream On" with its twisted Steven Tyler vocals. Jerry looks at us a little skeptically and asks if we've ever done this song before. "We can do it," Guy confidently responds for both of us.

Then we wait. A half an hour goes by and Guy settles into a restless funk. An hour goes by, others are singing their third or fourth songs, and Guy works through his frustration with whiskey and tobacco and muted insults of whoever's onstage. (On Steve's "Born to Be Wild": "He's tearin' this song to pieces." On Marney's "Arthur's Theme": "She screws up around here every time." On Mike's "Should I Stay or Should I Go": "Go, *go*.") One thing Guy doesn't do, though, is approach Jerry and ask him about our submission. Even as he pouts and sulks, he seems strangely resigned to being sidelined. (I am not so resigned, and when I put in for a solo take on "The Name Game," Jerry calls me up almost immediately.)

Jerry claims that if a patron whose slip he buried were to complain about it, he'd be obliged to let the person sing. "If they come up to me like, 'Hey, I put my slip in,' I'll let them go up again. I'm not gonna say no. That's just being cruel." Yet Guy doesn't complain, maybe because he senses that it's "for his own good." Though neither is eager to admit it, the performer may come to recognize the need for interdiction no less than the emcee. If this is deception, it's the knotty kind in which the deceiver is relatively benign and the deceived is silently, grudgingly complicit.[31]

Despite all attempts to dissuade or impede them, there will always be a complement of vocal eccentrics who insist on performing karaoke (and performing and performing), or it wouldn't be karaoke. When the real desperados make their way onstage, many emcees choose to sit by and let them fend for themselves. For the more interventionist emcees, though, this is precisely the time to pull out all the stops in their crisis management efforts. Some emcees will do whatever it takes to mediate aberrant performances and make them a functional part of the show rather than a disruption to it. Erving Goffman calls this "integration." "By contributing especially apt words and deeds, it is possible for a participant to blend . . . embarrassing matters smoothly into the encounter."[32] Sometimes emcees conspire with performers in this effort, sometimes they conspire with audience members, and sometimes they seem to operate on their own. However they act, they have to act with care since "an effort at integration that does not succeed ordinarily leaves matters in a worse state than before."[33] Emcees mobilize their knowledge of the crowd and their reading of the situation to intuit in hair-trigger fashion what others want or expect of them and what they can get away with.

One option is to team with the performer by offering back-channel assistance. The greatest challenge here may be ascertaining whether the performer wants help, or getting him to admit he needs it. "If they don't say anything and they're up there singing off key," says one emcee, "the question is, do you let them continue to sing off key and sound terrible, or do you do something to try to help them?" Emcees can step into the breach by whispering advice, or changing the key of the song, or changing the song altogether. The issue is whether and when and how to do so. They must take account of each singer's particular investment in his performance. With sensitive types, they must be more artful, casually offering and accepting excuses:

> During a break in the song, I might say to them, "Listen to the music, you're not paying attention to the music," and sometimes that will help them. I mean you're not gonna go up to them and say, "Excuse me, you're singing flat."

> If they're uptight about their singing, then even though you're on a familiar basis with them, you have to go, "You know what, Patty, that sounds a little high for you tonight. Your voice sounds a little strained. Why don't I bring that down a notch for you?" And normally, the singers you're familiar with know what you're doing, but you haven't embarrassed them. So they go, "Yeah, I have been talking a lot. Why don't you bring it down?" So I bring it down, start it over again, and it clicks.

I've seen a few emcees attempt something more emphatic. Like Cyrano feeding lines of verse to Christian, they stand behind performers and sing along without a microphone, just loud enough for performers to hear. Thus through tonometric feedback, they corral performers back on key. Yet here, emcees tread ever more lightly. As a performer, I can attest to the indignity of hearing someone over your shoulder meddling in what you thought was your brilliant improvisation.

Another option is for the emcee to team with the audience. Again, she positions herself behind or beside the performer, in this case exploiting her visual inaccessibility to the performer rather than her aural inaccessibility to the audience. One finds the odd emcee who takes pleasure in broadly grimacing or stuffing napkins in her ears behind the backs of certain hapless performers. More commonly, the emcee uses her position to spur positive expressions—expressions that the performer is led to believe he has earned on his own—by holding up "applause" signs, or broadly mock-clapping, or raising her palms upward in a "let's hear it" gesture. Either way, emcee and audience conspire. Whether by venting true feelings or fabricating false expressions, they verify for one another a disparity between feelings and expressions.

Then there is a third option. The emcee can "make the situation,"[34] bringing suppressed feelings out into the open by flatly critiquing or mocking performances. Even here, though, emcees are more methodical than they might appear. Consider the brinkmanship of Charlie Nance, who works the basement karaoke room at the Borderline, a popular dance club in downtown Philly. Charlie is a sharp-dressing, fast-talking young emcee who is atypical in just about every way. Where most emcees are white, Charlie is black, though he ministers to a mostly white crowd. Where most emcees (at least, among those with relevant experience) come to their work by way of musical careers, Charlie is a stand-up comic. Where most emcees perform at least a couple of songs themselves each night, Charlie has little interest in performing and instead gets his kicks wisecracking between performances. And where most emcees are studiously supportive, Charlie razzes and signifies his way through every show. If you refuse to sing at one of his shows, you're liable to be showered with chants of "Wimp! Wimp! Wimp!" If you agree to sing and you're a little out of tune, you're seen off with hosannas like "I bet you'll wake up tomorrow really happy you did that!" or "What the hell was that?"

In Charlie's view, overindulgent hosts engage in bad-faith karaoke; they deceive performers about their true abilities and browbeat audiences into sustaining the deception. "The thing with trying to encourage people too much," he says, "is you come off as being phony. You come off as being obsequious—a butt-licker, basically. Sometimes, somebody will suck and I'll say, 'Hey, the least you can do is clap.' But I try not to say, 'Hey, great job! That was really, really good! Don Pardo, tell him what he's won!' I try not to do that if they're not all that good, because people aren't stupid, they know somebody sucked when they sucked."

Charlie is surprisingly well regarded by other emcees who seem to admire his capacity to ride roughshod over singers whom they themselves feel obliged to tiptoe around. ("He's the greatest emcee I've ever seen," one local colleague declared.) Even more surprising is his popularity with patrons. Each week, the Borderline's effete, young clubbers trickle downstairs until the cozy karaoke space is jam-packed. Hipsters line up to play the target for Charlie's hazing and seem to relish his shtick the more it resembles a *Gong Show* revival. The fact that an emcee who so patently violates the "feeling rules" for his work could have such success is a reminder of how flexible role performance can be when put in the hands of actual persons. Doing justice to the artistry of emceeing, or of any service work, demands attention to workers' normative, typical, and individual role performance—respectively, how they're "supposed to" act, how most of them do act, and how only one or two of them may be crazy enough to act.[35]

On closer inspection, though, Charlie is as tactful as any emcee. When the occasion demands, he can stroke egos with the best of them, and as a comedian he has an uncanny sense of how tightly he can put the screws on any particular performer. "If somebody's trying to be serious, you can't make fun of them. If their countenance doesn't show a light-hearted attitude, you know that they're taking this seriously, and it's best not to mess with them. But if they don't seem to care one way or the other, if they're kind of nonchalant . . . they won't care if you make a little fun of them. So that's what I do. It's a judgment call." In the shadow of his wiseacre front, Charlie is mobile, mercurial. He dodges and weaves, allying himself with the audience one moment, with the singer the next. When I do "Little Red Corvette," he announces, "That was Prince as done by an accountant," but quickly adds, "Actually, I liked that one." Thus he confronts the oddity of a frumpish, white guy singing Prince, yet assuages me with a hasty thumbs-up.

And sometimes, with laser-guided sarcasm, he manages to ally himself with both sides at once. When I ask Charlie how he handles performers who have no idea how bad they are, he says, "I offer a sarcastic remark in total sincerity." I look at him quizzically. "It's a win-win situation," he adds. "The people that know I'm being facetious, they pick up on what I'm doing. And everybody else—well, if they don't know, they don't know." Later on, he gets a chance to prove his point. A young man named Millin takes the stage and solemnly declares, "I'd like to dedicate this song to my wife, Dana, on our third anniversary." He then erupts into a horrific dismemberment of the Diana Ross-Lionel Richie number, "Endless Love." The audience seems uncomfortable and unsure how to respond until the song ends and Charlie announces, in the broadest possible manner, "You know what? That was *so sweet!*" Sure enough, half the audience chuckles, the other half cheers, and Millin and Dana go home with the brightest smiles in town.

Critics of service work argue that, through compulsory emotional displays, workers become alienated from their emotions no less than physical laborers become alienated from their bodies. In this view, workers can either commit themselves to their work and sacrifice control of their feelings, or distance themselves from their work and sacrifice connection with their feeling displays. Yet emcees' experience on the job is far more complex than either of these options suggests. Most emcees are supportive in their dealings with customers, yet while their support is rarely wholly disingenuous, it is almost always measured and deliberate. Emcees are first and foremost neither sincere nor cynical, but strategic.

As Goffman teaches us, strategic interaction is endemic to modern life. Whenever we're less than wholly familiar with one another's statuses, opinions, or expectations, as we so often are in the public life of modern societies, we're forced to feel one another out through guarded disclosures. "One individual admits his views or statuses to another a little at a time. After dropping his guard just a little he waits for the other to show reason why it is safe for him to do this, and after this reassurance he can safely drop his guard a little bit more."[36] Organizational theorist Karl Weick refers to such exchanges as "double interacts": one person acts, another responds, and the first responds to the response.[37] It's the simplest exchange in the world, yet it's also the most complex, because by means of it we determine what roles we're to play, what selves we're to be.

Double interacts are legion in the emotional transactions of emcees, as of all service workers.[38] Emcees generously offer advice and commentary, but usually in ways that are tentative, equivocal, deniable. They constantly feel customers out, check their perceptions, express or withhold or fabricate emotions as each case demands. And they're no more slaves to their customers than to the feelings associated with their work. In fact, they often use emotional display to preserve a measure of status, control, and private sanity.

Emcee Performances

On the Pinocchio's Daring Journey attraction at Anaheim's Disneyland, guests watch as the thrill-seeking puppet is lured to Pleasure Island, where children eat candy apples and ride Ferris wheels all day only to be transformed into donkeys and sold for labor at night. Of all the "dark rides" at

Disneyland, Pinocchio's Daring Journey is surely the darkest. Like Disney's 1940 film and Carlo Collodi's 1883 children's story, the ride is a dystopian vision of what happens when pleasure becomes work, or when pleasure is force-fed so methodically that it comes to feel like work. And it's only made darker by the fact that its architects, who premiered the ride on the hundredth anniversary of Collodi's book, seem to have been oblivious to the twisted irony of its theme-park-within-a-theme-park. Perhaps customers better appreciate the irony since the ride's queue is routinely among the shortest in the park. And the park's line workers almost certainly appreciate it. Many theme park employees are drawn to their work after visiting the parks as guests or taking in their advertised mythos from afar. Prospective employees at Disney's Florida park, according to one study, often migrate to Orlando "with exceedingly high, perhaps naïve, expectations . . . that Disney must be 'the epitome of a fun place to work.'"[39] Lumbering along in overheated costumes for little more than minimum wage, workers can be forgiven for wondering if they're having fun yet.

Of course, the estrangement of working where others amuse themselves is not peculiar to Disney workers or to theme park workers. It's a feeling familiar to many workers in an economy increasingly driven by leisure and consumption. What Gross writes of modern arts institutions could as easily describe the ever-burgeoning field of "leisure services." Both are sites that "real people visit in their fringe, spare time, but only fringe, spare people inhabit in their real time."[40] Karaoke emcees' own daring journey often begins as performers, and while some come to karaoke with experience singing publicly, others bring only vague, persistent dreams of singing coupled with a learned sense that singing is not something real people do in their real time. Some of them latch onto karaoke as nothing short of paradise, and see emceeing as an opportunity not just to visit paradise but to live it. Inevitably, they find that emceeing is not at all like performing. Yet their biggest disappointment is not (as service work polemicists might predict) that they're forced to give so much support, but that they receive so little; it's not that they're "always onstage," but that they're not onstage enough. The emcee can become a sort of "nonperson," edged out of the heart of the show even as she carries it on her back.[41]

As keepers of the machines, emcees seem to be in an enviable position. At home, they can endlessly tinker and rehearse and delight in karaoke. But once the show gets going, like waiters or salespeople, they're expected to deliver the goods and not partake of them. Singing too much is the surest way for emcees to get on a crowd's bad side. "I don't want the emcee being the entertainment, I just want him moving things along," says a Philadelphia karaoke impresario. Another emcee goes as far as to say, "When I'm doing karaoke, I should be invisible." Even when emcees get requests to perform solo—as they now and then do, often from non-singing patrons—many force themselves to defer to singing patrons. The loss of singing opportunities is an endless source of frustration for those making the transition from performing to emceeing. "I'm just like everybody else," laments one host. "I like getting up to sing for the sheer pleasure of it. We don't really do that anymore."

I know the feeling, from my own first and last foray into emceeing. In April 1996, the chairperson of the department I teach for asks me to arrange a round of karaoke for our end-of-the-school-year soirée. I rent a topflight, portable system with all the extras (CD and graphics capability, key control, triple tray changer) and loads of software. On the premise of testing it out, I pick it up the evening before the party, hook it up to my TV set, and play with it for most of the night. Sitting there singing in my pajamas, I try several dozen songs. Partly, I'm rehearsing for tomorrow night's audience and prospecting for a few tunes that I can render adequately. But mostly I'm lost in a selfish reverie, transported to a karaoke Valhalla where I play emcee, performer, and audience—until, every so often, I raise my voice and fall to earth when the baby cries or my wife emerges bleary-eyed from the bedroom to shut me up.

The next night, after drinks and dinner and an hour or so of technical difficulties, I start the show. I open with the Everly Brothers' "All I Have to Do is Dream," and the novelty of karaoke and of me doing it is enough to win a warm ovation from my friends and colleagues. "Anybody else want to try this?" I ask, but they're not quite ready, and I'm not going to force them—I've got a half dozen more numbers I'm itching to do. I swagger through "Na Na Hey Hey Kiss Him Goodbye," and again they applaud but this time not so warmly. They've figured out where this is going and they begin volunteering if only to rein me in. The recondite cultural studies scholar does "You Light Up My Life"; the nationally known, organizational communication authority does "To Sir with Love." Soon they're amusing themselves quite capably, and my contribution is reduced to bumbling, between-song banter (which, in contrast to my singing, I haven't bothered to rehearse at all).

I smile and play my part, but feel vaguely bitter. I want to ask, "Would anyone mind doing this for awhile and letting me pretend that *you're* forcing *me* to sing?" In my pettiness, I resent others' freedom to perform as much as my own loss of it. I feel as though something's been usurped from me—the machine, the attention, the show itself. It's the same feeling I encounter a few months later, when my wife and I bring our eight-month-old on his first family vacation. Our relatives pass him around for much of the week, cooing and gurgling over him, insensible to our own desire to express and perform our affection for him. Now and then, we sneak in a hug and feel almost selfish. "You get to play with him all the time!" my niece complains. The life we've created is upstaging us. What we thought was ours, it now seems, is everyone else's.

I don't mean to suggest that emcees never get to sing. But when they do, it tends to be in a kind of sacrificial capacity. They're the ones who usually tackle the evening's first performance—to break the ice, but also (like a taste tester) to take the fall and make adjustments for any early audio problems. They're the ones expected to stand in when any singer requests vocal or moral assistance with any song (though they often "hang toward the back a bit" to avoid upstaging their customers). They're the ones who must do the busy work of singing when there are no volunteers and the place is dead, but must sit on the sidelines when there's a twenty-plus rotation and the place is rocking.

Emcees also feel obligated to maintain a certain decorum in their performances. Once they take the stage, they assume all the liabilities of "role models." There are onstage pleasures that are central to karaoke, but that emcees—whose audiences may range from head bangers to Bible-thumpers—don't want to be seen as encouraging. They're likely to avoid some of the spicier tunes in their repertoires. "Certain songs I just won't do when I'm working. Like, I don't normally do 'Like a Virgin' anymore. It just doesn't work with the image." ("Like a Virgin" is positively virginal compared to the mother lodes of explicit lyrics available on some karaoke lists, from Nine Inch Nails's "Closer" to Adam Sandler's "Ode to My Car" to Snoop Dogg's "What's My Name?") They also avoid the sort of kicking and screaming that lends force to popular musical performance but could pose a danger to self, others, and equipment. And, of course, they avoid any appearance of drunkenness. In karaoke's early days, when it was at its most thrilling and terrifying, the emcees often seemed to be, along with the bartenders, bouncers, and designated drivers, among the only sober ones in the house.

There's another risk emcees face onstage, one shared by all workers who offer themselves as examples to customers. Their performances can spark jealousy and rivalry. It's a situation familiar to the willowy, young saleswomen at the upscale Paris boutiques observed by Henri Peretz. Though they're required to wear the store's clothing on the job, Peretz finds it can complicate their relationships with customers and undermine their sales. Size-twelve customers insist on wriggling into the saleswoman's size-ten dresses; older customers covet her youthful, flowered blouses and denim skirts. Sometimes, "the customer seems to want to appropriate for herself the saleswoman's looks," and sometimes the saleswoman's looks are enough to cast a gloom over the customer's entire shopping spree. Peretz finds that many of the stores' habituées prefer dealing with the gay male sales staff, who present themselves not as models but as fawning advisors.[42]

In the same way, bar customers are liable to take emcees' performances as indicators of karaoke's baseline vocal requirements. Some emcees feel a need to downplay their singing ability—what Goffman calls "negative idealization."[43] To reassure customers and preserve karaoke's spirit of inclusiveness, they must make it look easy without making themselves look too deft: "If you're too good as a host, you intimidate people. But if you suck, people are like, 'Oh my God, she can't even sing and she owns [the equipment], I'm not doing it!'" Again, there's a cruel irony here. Many emcees are skilled vocalists who bring a passion for singing to their work, yet they're obliged to conceal this very skill. One emcee I knew would dazzle audiences at other emcees' shows with majestic ballads by Jeffrey Osborne and Phil Collins, yet he opened his own shows with "Mary Had a Little Lamb." "There are songs in the book that just sort of drag but that are good demonstration songs, because the words come across the screen real slow," he told me. Thus, emcee performances tend to be bland and methodical, demonstrating how karaoke works without calling attention to themselves.

A final difference in emcees' experience as performers is that they consistently receive less applause than other singers receive. Thus they're shortchanged, not only of opportunities to sing and display competence, but also of the recognition and ego enhancement that other singers receive so amply. When an emcee takes center stage, awkwardly introducing her own song or, just as awkwardly, breaking into song without introduction, customers sometimes seem to treat it as an imprimatur to shirk the basic formalities of audience behavior. They might tune her out or they might coolly tolerate her, but they're unlikely to greet her with any enthusiasm.

Emcees are distressed by this lack of response and struggle to account for it. Often they feel they're taken for granted or envied or resented for singing at all. Yet such explanations point to a larger dynamic between emcees and customers. The circumstances seem to breed an attitude of selfishness in customers toward their hosts. The more strenuously emcees applaud customers' performances, the more studiously customers seem to ignore emcees' own performances. Recall that many emcees are female, and that emcees' transactions with customers often require them to behave and be treated in ways that are culturally coded as feminine. Here, then, we find that emcees are hemmed into a position of emotional self-sufficiency that parallels women's role expectations within families—where, feminist psychoanalyst Nancy Chodorow famously argues, "men are socially and psychologically reproduced by women, but women are reproduced (or not) largely by themselves."[44]

If the experience of unreciprocated emotional support is probably more familiar to female emcees, it is more jarring to males. For men, emotionally demanding forms of service work such as that performed by emcees are "gender atypical." Male emcees learn the hard way what it's like to bear the burden of nurturing others, and what it's like to get by on precious little nurturance in return. Take, for example, Dan Kane, a Philadelphia emcee who, with his wife and business partner, Lori, is among my closest friends in karaoke circles. Dan began emceeing after earning his M.B.A., and in our early talks he seems to view it as a purely impersonal, business venture. He often expresses his hopes for karaoke's continued growth and his dreams of putting together a larger operation. He is hard working and driven, constantly scouting for gigs, bargaining with bar owners, and keeping books.

Yet I can't help feeling that Dan gets more out of karaoke than he lets on. In describing his first encounter with karaoke, he assumes an almost evangelical tone. On their honeymoon in Florida, he and Lori happened upon the karaoke show at their hotel lounge and wound up spending the next three evenings there. They met another couple and started doing quartets with them. The emcee gave out tapes of performances, and the other couple had a Walkman with some miniature speakers. "We went out and got some beer and went to the outdoor Jacuzzi, and set the little speakers up. And we sat there, and drank, and listened to our songs, and laughed our little tails off." Drunk on beer and song and laughter, it occurred to Dan and Lori that they might do this for a living.

Though Lori does more of the talking at shows, Dan does more of the performing. (Lori is self-effacing about her singing: "I'm not billed as the singer. He is, I'm not.") And it is as a performer that Dan betrays an investment in karaoke that is something other than monetary. He is one of the most dedicated performers I've encountered. He rehearses obsessively and when he takes the stage a look of utter resoluteness comes over him. He delights in recounting certain peak performances, like the time he first went out with his supplier and emceeing mentor, Ray. It was back in karaoke's early days when volunteers were hard to come by, and Ray asked Dan to play the shill and spark the show:

> Ray told me, "Dan, why don't you put a slip in, get things going, 'cause they think you're part of the audience." As soon as he said, "Now Dan's gonna come up here, we've got our first singer," everybody stopped what they were doing to see who's the fool who's gonna get up there and sing. And I got up there and they were all eyes on me—quiet, man, in a club where people had been drinking and going nuts, right? And I sang that song, and by God, I thought they were gonna attack me when I was done. They were freaking out, on their feet, man.

It is in the context of Dan's complicated relationship with karaoke that the following exchange takes place. We are talking about the differences between emceeing and performing when, out of the blue, Dan remarks, "See, I don't get much crowd response. I'm not saying it never happens, but it seems like when I sing, people don't clap afterwards."

"They don't want to feed his ego," says Lori.

"I'm not sure what it is," Dan says. "Maybe they just figure, 'He's supposed to be good, we don't need to clap for him.'"

"Because it didn't take guts for him to do what he just did," Lori says.

"Right, it didn't take guts for me to do that. No risk, I do it all the time, I'm supposed to be good. Now, the next guy that comes up can be horrible, and boy, these people will be on their feet giving him an ovation. 'Cause I'm not one of them now, see? I'm the guy running the show. I'm not the guy in the audience."

"That's interesting," I say. "Do you ever feel sort of left out in a way?"

Dan thinks. "Um . . ."

"Yeah, you do," says Lori.

"Yeah," says Dan. "Because you know you did a good job on it, and you're thinking to yourself, 'Gee, out of common courtesy they could clap, even if they do have this image of me.' See, an audience has responsibilities, too. Audiences have to respond even if someone's bad. I'm talking about karaoke now, not a professional situation. Audiences have responsibilities, and I think when I get up to sing, just to do the first song, they should respond accordingly as an audience, because I performed for them and I'm entitled to something."

"Often, I'll get on the microphone and I'll say, 'You know, you're allowed to clap for Dan,'" says Lori.

"And then they'll clap," says Dan.

"Sometimes," says Lori.

"But doesn't it seem like maybe they don't feel that same responsibility with you, that they feel with other people?" I ask.

"Right," says Lori, "they don't think he needs the reinforcement. Because I'll tell you what, after he sings and they don't clap, Dan will always come up to me at least once and say, 'Well, how was that? Did I sound all right on that song? Did I screw it up? Was I okay?' Because he wants to know that he did a good job."

Aside from Dan's obvious despair over his listeners' negligence, what's most provocative here is the dynamic between Dan and Lori. The crowd's response to Lori's rare performances is never an issue, in this or any of our other conversations. Instead, Lori plays the role of both emcee and audience for Dan. She rouses listeners to applaud him, and when he needs to be told that he "sounded all right," he turns to her. Many times during our talks, Lori finds opportunities to praise Dan's vocal ability. These karaoke honeymooners seem to have elevated performing and applauding to a sustaining ritual of their relationship, yet they've worked it out in a way that precisely mirrors traditional gender arrangements.

Maybe everyone needs somewhere they can go to be coddled with the milk and honey of unconditional support. The women in Janice Radway's classic study of romance reading find it in their Harlequins and Silhouettes, which evoke "a figurative journey to a utopian state of total receptiveness where the reader, as a result of her identification with the heroine, feels herself the *object* of someone else's attention."[45] Emcees (both male and female) who haven't the benefit of all-providing partners often find it at colleagues' shows. "When I start to feel burnt out it is usually because I feel unappreciated," writes one emcee in an Internet discussion. "So I go karaoke somewhere new or somewhere I haven't been in a while. People love to hear a good voice, you get the pats on the back you miss, and you remember why you do karaoke for a living."[46]

Unconditional support . . . I wonder sometimes where Lori Kane finds it, and when I think of how steadfastly my own loving partner has stood by to quell my excessive hang-ups about this very book, I wonder where she finds it, too.

CHAPTER SIX
GOOD, OLD KARAOKE

Acentury and a half ago, we're often told, singing was at the center of social life. The piano was a fixture and the sing-along a sustaining ritual of middle-class homes. Choral societies dotted the nation. Regional and subcultural song forms flourished. People sang at school, at work, at worship. Yet in our own time, public singing has become a rarity for many of us, limited to clumsy iterations of "Happy Birthday" and "Auld Lang Syne." This dearth of singing has been blamed on the spread of recording, the professionalization of amateur activities, the plundering of folk musical forms by commercial interests, the star system, cuts in music education, copyright laws, cabaret laws, and cultural stratification. While there's evidence pointing to all these causes, as much as anything, it seems to come down to our own feelings of vocal inadequacy, as well as our vague sense that music making is alien to the real business of life.[1]

Yet the story has never been that simple. There have always been those who refused to stay seated in the audience, who sang against the silence. Now, right on time for the new millennium, comes something else entirely. Through digital wizardry, the words of the most commercialized songs are stolen from the mouths of the stars and yielded to us, the listeners, challenging us to bring them back to performance and back to life. Naturally, many of us assume it's a joke. Skeptics can dismiss karaoke performers as star-struck parrots or stardom-obsessed peacocks, but there's no getting around one thing: people are singing where they weren't before. Selves are taking shape, lives are interconnecting. Public life is happening where it wasn't before; where there was silence, there is now speech. But does karaoke really signify a meaningful, sustainable change in music making? Might it be one way of returning singing to its rightful place at the

119

center of life and consciousness? Or is it a fad that will soon join the scrap heap of derelict commercial culture? What challenges lie ahead if karaoke is to flourish? What might karaoke herald for cultural and social life?

Though public karaoke remains popular, for it to thrive it will have to remain profitable as well. Karaoke occupies a precarious position in the U.S. nightlife economy. Participants rarely pay for it directly; most often, it is sponsored by bar owners who pass its costs on to customers via drink prices. Thus despite emcees' constant entreaties to "support the bar," performers tend to experience karaoke as "free." Of course, it isn't free, and although it's built for survival—small scale, cheap, and portable—its future will depend in part on whether bar owners continue to see it as lucrative. It may not help matters that karaoke's habitués have acquired a reputation as teetotalers. When karaoke first became popular, most performers needed a few doses of liquid courage before even approaching the mike. Nowadays, though, many seasoned performers avoid alcohol in order to maintain clear voices and clear heads. (One performer I met would arrive at the bar toting a thermos of licorice and slippery elm tea.) Bar owners sometimes see this as a drawback of karaoke, and a few have resorted to cover charges or drink minimums, yet it's unclear whether or not customers will be willing to pay for karaoke up front. Like the sponsors of that other new medium of the 1990s—the Internet—some bar owners have come to regret the build-it-and-they-will-come ebullience with which they initially embraced karaoke.

Other routes for karaoke's future expansion may lie beyond the bars. There's always been a non-bar market for karaoke operations (particularly at private parties), and as Americans have grown more accustomed to karaoke, they've become more willing to invite it into the spaces of their daily lives. Grade schools, senior centers, social clubs, and places of worship all provide opportunities for institutional support and daytime gigs for karaoke operators.[2] At some point, too, karaoke may catch on in a freestanding format, as it has throughout Asia with the spread of semiprivate "karaoke rooms." While karaoke may seem inseparable from the drunken swirl of the bar context, nothing about the technology dictates this. Even the early nickelodeons were improvised in rented storefronts, arcades, and restaurants before they became housed in independent theaters.[3]

Yet karaoke's spread to more discrete, semiprivate venues and clienteles raises another question: will it continue to facilitate diverse, public communication as it has in the bars? Karaoke's eclecticism has always engendered a certain discomfort. Emcees' lore is full of horror stories such as the one of the young goths who show up at the piano bar gig and stun the crowd by slipping a Marilyn Manson tune in between Sinatra and Peggy Lee. Already, the balkanizing language of the niche marketer is making its way into karaoke circles, spurred in part by the increasing availability of genre-specific software: "Assuming your goal is to establish a for-profit karaoke service, the first thing to ask yourself is, 'Who am I going to charge for my service?' If you are going to entertain nursing home patients, a headbanger [karaoke software] series just wouldn't be appropriate!"[4] Perhaps someday soon, no karaoke audience will ever need to suffer through another performance that isn't tailored to its demographic. Yet part of karaoke's wonder is that it's *not* just an in-group phenomenon. Karaoke isn't just about validating personal and social identities, it's about performing and testing these identities before others. Hopefully it will maintain its noisy heterogeneity, its potential for diverse genres and communities to rub up against one another.

The larger threat to karaoke's diversity will come not from demographic division, but from division between the classically talented vocalists and the rest of us. As people become more serious about karaoke, as they invest more time and effort (and, in some cases, money) in it, they become less patient with its free-for-all atmosphere and more concerned with standards.[5] Talented singers who seek out worthy rivals and discerning listeners converge on certain bars. These bars become known for high standards; some people attend them just to watch, others who might be inclined to sing are often cowed by the competition. A sharper divide thus sets in between performers and audiences. Some emcees, too, come to see the talent level as a factor in their shows' popularity and rig the rotation in favor of the local prodigies. A few observers even advocate devoting a portion of karaoke shows to polished routines by professionals or skilled amateurs: "Not only are you guaranteed they know how to sing, but are use to [*sic*] singing on stage, therefore able to be more entertaining than the average karaoke customer."[6]

This emphasis on singing quality also accounts for the increasing prevalence of contests in karaoke bars. Bars like contests because they draw crowds and fill the tills. Performers will travel long distances for them (often with friends in tow), lured by the thrill of competition, the prospect of cash prizes, and the opportunity to sing in front of large audiences. Contests tend to be hyped-up, tense affairs; nerves are jangled and must be calmed with a ready supply of alcohol. Increasingly, local contests are affiliated with regional or national tournaments sponsored by karaoke hardware and software companies. Such tournaments serve as a form of "event marketing" for the companies; they're promoted heavily and often draw local press coverage. Often, the participants in these contests are anything but hobbyists. Many are trained singers who are looking to "take it to the next level" and see karaoke as one more opportunity to "get noticed."

Contests occasion a good deal of debate in karaoke circles. Bar regulars complain that they draw "professional contestants" who (like one character in the karaoke-themed movie *Duets*) roam from bar to bar hustling for prize money. Nonregulars complain that they're often rigged in favor of regulars. What's undeniable is that contests change the spirit of karaoke. At a tournament-affiliated contest I attend in Florida, one link in a long series of rounds within and beyond the bar, this change is apparent. The bar is packed with spectators whose attention is focused resolutely on the stage. There's an edgy seriousness to the proceedings. The crowd busts out in applause on cue after each performance, but otherwise they're remarkably quiet. Three judges sit stony-faced in front of the stage, their movements monitored almost as closely as the performers. The performers are all marvelous. A man who's adorned half his body with a dress, a wig, and makeup does a hilarious version of the *Grease* duet, "Summer Lovin'," turning this way and that for the male and female parts. A man in a double-breasted suit with an open shirt collar delivers Lou Rawls's "You'll Never Find Another Love Like Mine" with the campy panache of a seventies supper club singer. A woman in a tie-dyed shirt emblazoned with a peace sign does a frenzied rendition of "Piece of My Heart" that would give Janis Joplin a run.

Watching such contests, I inevitably find my reference points shifting from the easygoing, convivial world of karaoke to the winner-take-all world of pop stardom. I wonder who among the contestants could deliver under a television camera's stare or within the cloistered severity of a recording studio. Some of them occasionally slip off-key or flub a line. Some are a little short or heavy or old or plain looking. Only one young woman seems like star material. She's dressed to the nines in a long red gown, with the all-American looks and easy smile of a prom queen. She sings Whitney Houston's "One Moment in Time," an eighties paean to determination and perseverance and following your dreams that's capacious and cliché-ridden enough to offer something for everybody. She tosses it off in a clear, supple voice interlaced with showy cadenzas in the manner of Houston, Mariah Carey, and a hundred other such divas. When she once or twice misses a note by a hair, she continues as if nothing had happened, betraying not a hint of self-doubt. Her performance is so flawless that I have no idea what she's thinking. And, of course, she takes first place. The contenders are weeded out, the social ideal emerges, and we have a winner.

It's pointless to argue against a certain degree of bifurcation between performers and audiences in karaoke. There's an appeal in giving oneself up to the artistry of great singers in karaoke bars no less than anywhere else. (There's also, sometimes, a mischievous glee in watching them wrestle with the key and tempo and TelePrompTed lyrics of the karaoke tracks, just like the rest of us.) The danger, particularly with contests, is that karaoke stops functioning as democratic speech, the hip-hop of middle-aged, middle-class Americans. Though contests supposedly take all comers, it's hard not to feel excluded if you're an unexceptional vocalist. What communication researchers call a "spiral of silence" kicks in. I wouldn't think of entering a contest like that described above, or even taking the stage when the format shifts to open mike afterward. Moreover, as soon as objective standards are applied to karaoke, the question arises: whose standards? Though a variety of performers may enter the contests, the ones who usually win are the balladeers and crooners, the ones who most closely match the cultural ideal of good singing. (As at the Oscars and Grammys, comedians don't quite cut it, nor do eccentrics or provocateurs.) At its best, karaoke's joys are serendipitous; there are wonderful singers, and there are terrible singers who are wonderful in their own ways. They're like the joys of watching Elvis in late career, when, as Mojo Nixon once said, you could see "the coolest thing and the schlockiest thing in the same five minutes."[7] My hope is that karaoke will never lose the unpredictability that makes it more alive, more like life, than the bloodless perfectionism of most mass entertainment.

In all of this, I've made certain assumptions. I've assumed that if karaoke's profitability or diversity or inclusiveness could be assured, it would be relatively easy. I've assumed that if the software companies and the bar owners and the emcees act in karaoke's best interests, its base supporters will be able to carry on happily. I've assumed that karaoke can be, or should be, a normal, everyday activity. Yet it's hard not to feel that there's something excessive and off kilter at the heart of karaoke—a difference that can't be assimilated, a desire that can't be sated. Emerging bleary-eyed from a really good night of karaoke—singing in the street, dancing, mostly laughing—it's hard to make sense of what you've been through, but it isn't everyday and it isn't particularly normal.

It's tempting to see in karaoke (as, for instance, folklorist Don Cusic sees in it) the hope of a return to traditional, participatory modes of singing—the sorts of practices vaguely labeled as "folk singing."[8] Yet whatever karaoke strives toward, it's not the "folk" form of music making represented by a pub sing-along or a Christmas carol or a field holler or a lullaby. The fact that karaoke feeds on recorded, commercial music may be the least of the differences. Where folksinging is routine, karaoke is compulsive. Toward the end of a fevered karaoke session, even regulars can be heard to clamor for one last turn at the mike. As with problem gambling, "Unless you're painfully aware that you walked away from the table too late, you're bound to wonder whether you walked away too soon."[9] And if it's unsatisfying to sit by and watch, it's often only slightly more satisfying to go up and sing. Where folksinging is mundane and functional, karaoke is fanciful, otherworldly. Some of the dreams performers confess to are as unlikely as anything out of Nancy Friday: singing naked, singing alongside favorite pop stars, singing at high school reunions, singing to lovers they've yet to meet.[10] Karaokists can readily sympathize with Marilyn Monroe's admission, "Dreaming of people looking at me made me feel less lonely."[11]

And where folksinging is stable and synergetic, karaoke is stubbornly individualistic and starved for attention. While I've only encountered one singer who warned her audience before each performance, "Don't sing while I'm singing," I've heard others express similar sentiments privately. Even when they sing in groups, celebrating and solidifying personal relationships, karaoke performers are driven to make those relationships public, to open them up to the world. Even when they sing the same old songs to the same old crowd week after week, they often thrive on the hope for new listeners. While practically every performer has his "home bar" (the place where, when you have to go there, they have to take you in), many refuse to stay put at their home bars and will trek for miles in pursuit of virgin audiences.

Karaoke, then, is not normal—yet its abnormality hails a whole new world. Rather than a premodern, folk mode of music making, karaoke points to a fully modern mode, one that comes to terms with our implacable drive for individual agency, creativity, and pleasure in modern society. At the time I first encountered karaoke, I was reading Jacques Attali's *Noise: The Political Economy of Music*.[12] It's a great read, a sweeping survey of a thousand years of Western music written in the millenarian strains of continental theory. Attali limns a succession of four musical "networks," a term that encompasses practices, structures, and functions. The medieval world had a network of "sacrifice." Music produced by itinerant minstrels was an active part of daily life and ritual. Like sacrifice and religion in general, it functioned to sublimate violence and reconcile people to the social order. With the Renaissance came a second network of "representation." Music became a commodity enshrined within concert halls and silently witnessed by spectators. Rather than a ritual sacrifice, it functioned as a distant representation of social harmony. The twentieth century and the age of recording have begotten a third network of "repetition." Music is mass-produced by technicians and drained of all human qualities. Demand is sustained with brutal efficiency through the media, the pop charts, and the star system. Music no longer works as ritual or representation; it only isolates listeners and silences all competing noise. For Attali, music is heraldic; each network of music presages a new social and political order. Representation's spectacle of harmonic music foreshadowed larger ideologies of social harmony through representative government, scientific progress, and the free market. Repetition's mass-produced music heralded a dystopia where everything is mass-produced and a monopoly on noise and speech is cornered by faceless institutions.

Up to this point, Attali's account of music history is no less gloomy than the accounts of many other mass cultural critics, if considerably more nuanced. But unlike those often nostalgic critics, Attali sees that there's no turning back. He envisions a fourth network: "complex, vague, recuperated, clumsy attempts to create new status for music—*not a new music, but a new way of making music*—are today radically upsetting everything music has been up to this point."[13] This utopian, future network, which

Attali refers to as "composition," "takes the route of the permanent affirmation of the right to be different . . . the conquest of the right to make noise . . . the right to compose one's life."[14] In this network, there would be no musicians or auditors, for everyone would make music and everyone would listen, as "to listen to music in the network of composition is to rewrite it."[15] There would be no concert halls or recording studios, no cloistered sites of music, "it is to be produced everywhere it is possible to produce it, in whatever way it is wished, by anyone who wants to enjoy it."[16] And there would be no profit or purpose in music. "It would be performed for the musician's own enjoyment, as self-communication, with no other goal than his own pleasure. . . . In this network, what is heard by others would be a by-product of what the composer or interpreter wrote or performed for the sake of hearing it."[17]

"As with all good French critical theory, the clarity is inseparable from the delirium," Greil Marcus writes of Attali's book.[18] After all Attali has written about it, it's difficult to say what a musical network of composition would sound like. He offers only a few, sketchy bits of evidence: the alternative musical network of free jazz, the resurgence in new instrument production, the mushrooming of local bands. It may seem unlikely to hold karaoke up as an exemplar of "composition." Certainly, it's hard to imagine Attali giving karaoke any serious consideration, in view of his antipathy for most of the commercial, popular music on which karaoke is founded (though he does give a nod to the protokaraoke Music Minus One for "allowing one to insinuate oneself into production").[19] Yet so much about karaoke resonates with Attali's account of composition: its inclusiveness, its situational flexibility, its potential for improvisation and play, and most of all, its striving for autonomous pleasure. In the end, karaoke is about pleasure, the pure, physical pleasure of singing, the pleasure of assuming the guises embodied by songs and succumbing to the emotions aroused by songs. It's about pleasure in difference, in the body, in the self—"an empowered self who gifts the pleasure of performance to others."[20] And, like Attali's composition, karaoke epitomizes not just a way of making music but a way of life. The pure, sheer joy of song casts a model for how we can live every moment of every day. Utopian, cobbled together from impossible dreams, karaoke gropes toward a space where we can all take and give pleasure openly and unashamedly yet in ways we all can live with. This is the world that karaoke begs, but short of such a world, one wonders if karaoke can ever be all that we want it to be.

Sometimes late at night, I lie on the couch with my headphones on and I sing. This was the impetus for our white noise machine, which we bought to drown out my own decidedly off-white noise. When I sing I'm given to fantasies, and nowadays my fantasies inevitably land me on a karaoke stage. Sometimes the song I'm singing is half directed toward certain intimates I imagine are in the crowd, to whom I'd like to say something or wish I'd said something: Def Leppard's "Armageddon It" to impress my brothers, They Might Be Giants's "Birdhouse in Your Soul" to celebrate the quirky chemistry I share with my wife, the Carpenters's "Close to You" to let my older son know what his blue eyes do to me. Other times, the song's for anyone who will listen, something I've wanted to air, a cry of discontent or a call to arms: Midnight Oil's "The Dead Heart," Elvis Costello's "The Other Side of Summer," or Iris DeMent's "Wasteland of the Free." Most of the time, the song's just for me, something solitary and egotistical, a meditation or a confession, something that might not appear on any karaoke list and that I wouldn't sing publicly if it did: Moby Grape's "Naked If I Want To," Olivia Newton-John's "Have You Never Been Mellow," Steely Dan's "Deacon Blues," the Fastbacks's "Three Boxes," Kathy Mattea's "Knee Deep In a River," or the Pretenders's "Night in My Veins."

As I sing, a feeling comes over me now and then that's hard to describe, a feeling that slips into fakery as easily as descriptions of it slip into triteness. Singing someone else's song, maybe one I've sung many times before, it suddenly feels (even as it trips off my tongue) like I've never sung it before, like no one's ever sung it before. I feel rooted by the words and music, utterly centered and self-contained, even with all eyes upon me. I look at the audience almost as an afterthought, and they're as caught up in it as I am, and I draw on their excitement, and they draw on mine. To find the joy at the heart of a song, to let others witness my joy so they feel it too, to feel their eyes on me so the joy's only greater, to make songs come alive every day the way they were meant to. No longer having to hide, I'm fully myself at such moments, suddenly knowing for sure who I am.

I open my eyes. I'm still on the living room couch, still in the dark, still in my pajamas. And my own peak karaoke performances, I'm afraid, still begin and end right here.

NOTES

Prologue

1. John Lofland and Lyn H. Lofland, *Analyzing Social Settings*, 2d ed. (Belmont, Calif.: Wadsworth, 1984), 7.

2. Karaoke enthusiasts often refer to the people who run their shows as "karaoke jockeys" or "kayjays." For simplicity's sake, I'll use the more generic term "emcee" throughout.

3. Leroi Jones, "Minton's," in *Black Music* (New York: William Morrow, 1967).

Chapter 1

1. On karaoke's history, see Toru Mitsui, "The Genesis of Karaoke: How the Combination of Technology and Music Evolved," in *Karaoke Around the World: Global Technology, Local Singing*, ed. Toru Mitsui and Shuhei Hosokawa (New York: Routledge, 1998). On karaoke at MIT and Oxford, see, respectively, "MIT Research Pushes Sound Standard for Personal Computers, Internet to New Level," *MIT News*, 8 April 1998, <http://web.mit.cdu/newsoffice/nr/1998/websound.html> [accessed 29 March 2000]; and Nigel Hawkes, "Karaoke Kings Can Now Step into Elvis's Blue Suede Shoes," *Times* (London), 19 March 1998. On punk karaoke, see Jennifer Poyen, "Punk Posers: Nihilists Go on a Rant at One-Time Karaoke Night," *San Diego Union-Tribune*, 16 February 1999. On "The Karaoke Sound of Music," see Rhoda Koenig, "'The Karaoke Sound of Music' Has Audiences Singing Along," *Wall Street Journal*, 21 January 2000. On Kosovar karaoke, see Nina Teicholz, "A Wide-Eyed American Engineers the First Karaoke Airlift," *New Yorker*, 21 June 1999.

2. "U.S.A. Sings," *Jolt Online Karaoke Forum*, 27 May 1998, <http://jolt.karaoke.com/jolt?14@^131126@.ee6c9e6> [accessed 3 March 2000].

3. Hiroshi Ogawa, "The Effects of Karaoke on Music in Japan," in *Karaoke around the World*, 47; Steve McClure, "Karaoke Japan," *Billboard*, 25 June 1994, 78.

4. Robert C. Toll, *The Entertainment Machine: American Show Business in the Twentieth Century* (New York: Oxford University Press, 1982), 100–104; Lawrence W. Levine, "The Sacralization of Culture," in *Highbrow/Lowbrow: The Emergence of Cultural Hierarchy in America* (Cambridge, Mass.: Harvard University Press, 1988), 139–40; Richard Butsch, introduction to *For Fun and Profit: The Transformation of Leisure into Consumption*, ed. Richard Butsch (Philadelphia: Temple University Press, 1990), 14–19; Michael Kammen, *American Culture, American Tastes* (New York: Knopf, 1999), 22–26.

5. Simon Frith, "Art versus Technology: The Strange Case of Popular Music," *Media, Culture, and Society* 8 (1986): 272–77; Steve Jones, *Rock Formation: Music, Technology, and Mass Communication* (Newbury Park, Calif.: Sage, 1992), 137–43; Charles Keil, "Music Mediated and Live in Japan," in *Music Grooves*, ed. Charles Keil and Steven Feld (Chicago: University of Chicago Press, 1994).

6. Sara Cohen, *Rock Culture in Liverpool: Popular Music in the Making* (New York: Oxford University Press, 1991), 103–4; Barry Shank, *Dissonant Identities: The Rock 'n' Roll Scene in Austin, Texas* (Hanover, N.H.: Wesleyan University Press, 1994), 162–237.

7. Toru Mitsui and Shuhei Hosokawa, introduction to *Karaoke Around the World*, 16–20.

8. Joshua Gamson, *Claims to Fame: Celebrity in Contemporary America* (Berkeley: University of California Press, 1994), 15–54; Neil Gabler, *Life: The Movie: How Entertainment Conquered Reality* (New York: Knopf, 1998), 143–91.

9. Simon Frith, "Video Pop: Picking Up the Pieces," in *Facing the Music*, ed. Simon Frith (New York: Pantheon, 1988), 110–14; Lawrence Grossberg, "You [Still] Have to Fight for Your Right to Party: Music Television as Billboards of Post-Modern Difference," *Popular Music* 7 (1988): 318; Mark Olson, "'Everybody Loves Our Town': Scenes, Spatiality, Migrancy," in *Mapping the Beat: Popular Music and Contemporary Theory*, ed. Thomas Swiss, John Sloop, and Andrew Herman (Malden, Mass.: Blackwell), 270–75.

10. P. David Marshall, *Celebrity and Power: Fame in Contemporary Culture* (Minneapolis: University of Minnesota Press, 1997), 246.

11. Richard Schickel, *Intimate Strangers: The Culture of Celebrity* (Garden City, N.Y.: Doubleday, 1985), 263. Also see Stuart Ewen, *All Consuming Images: The Politics of Style in Contemporary Culture* (New York: Basic, 1988), 91–101; and Cintra Wilson, "Magnificent Obsession," *Utne Reader*, May–June 2000.

12. Geoff Dyer, *Out of Sheer Rage* (London: Abacus, 1998), 78.

13. Mike Redmond, "Karaoke Fans Capable of Killing More Than Tunes," *Indianapolis Star*, 16 December 1998, sec. E, p. 1.

14. David Zimmerman, "Mindy McCready's One-Year Trek to Stardom," *USA Today*, 17 September 1996; Jerry Crowe, "The Teen Chart Queen," *Los Angeles Times*, 13 February 1996; Luke Fisher, "See Me, Feel Me, Touch Me," *Maclean's*, 6 March 1995.

15. Thomas A. Gonda Jr., "Cattle Call—Karaoke as Audition," in *Karaoke: The Bible*, ed. Thomas A. Gonda Jr. (Oakland, Calif.: G-Man Publishers, 1993).

16. Ruth Finnegan, *The Hidden Musicians: Music-Making in an English Town* (New York: Cambridge University Press, 1989); Cohen, *Rock Culture*; Shank, *Dissonant Identities*.

17. Erving Goffman, *Frame Analysis* (New York: Harper and Row, 1974), 124–55.

18. Cohen, *Rock Culture*, 85.

19. Paul Fussell, *Class: A Guide Through the American Status System* (New York: Simon & Schuster, 1983), 29–30.

20. Robert A. Stebbins, *Amateurs, Professionals, and Serious Leisure* (Montreal: McGill-Queen's University Press, 1992), 55.

21. Cf. Henry Jenkins, *Textual Poachers: Television Fans and Participatory Culture* (New York: Routledge, 1992), 9–12.

22. Raymond Williams, "Culture Is Ordinary," in *Resources of Hope: Culture, Democracy, Socialism* (London: Verso, 1988); Paul Willis, *Common Culture: Symbolic Work at Play in the Everyday Cultures of the Young* (Boulder, Colo.: Westview, 1990).

23. "Excerpts from Bush Speech at Rally," *New York Times*, 18 August 1992.

24. Quoted in William H. Kelly, "The Adaptability of Karaoke in the United Kingdom," in *Karaoke around the World*, 100 n.

25. Christine Yano, "The Floating World of Karaoke in Japan," *Popular Music and Society* 20 (1996): 1.

26. Goffman, *Frame Analysis*.

27. Deena Weinstein, "The History of Rock's Pasts through Rock Covers," in *Mapping the Beat*, 138.

28. Yano, "Floating World of Karaoke," 12. See also William H. Kelly, "Japan's Empty Orchestras: Echoes of Japanese Culture in the Performance of Karaoke," in *The Worlds of Japanese Popular Culture*, ed. D. P. Martinez (New York: Cambridge University Press, 1998), 80; Keil, "Music Mediated and Live," 252–53; Mitsui and Hosokawa, introduction to *Karaoke*, 13–14.

29. Yano, "Floating World of Karaoke," 2–4; Sepp Linhart, introduction to *The Culture of Japan as Seen through Its Leisure*, ed. Sepp Linhart and Sabine Frühstück (Albany, N.Y.: SUNY Press, 1998), 12.

30. Don F. Draeger, *Classical Budô* (New York: Weatherhill, 1973), 49; Eugen Herrigel, *Zen in the Art of Archery* (New York: Vintage, 1971), 45.

31. Michael Polanyi, *Personal Knowledge* (Chicago: University of Chicago Press, 1958), 53.

32. Kelly, "Japan's Empty Orchestras," 86 n.

33. Kunihiro Narumi, "The Electric Geisha," in *The Electric Geisha: Exploring Japan's Popular Culture*, ed. Atsushi Ueda (New York: Kodansha International, 1994), 65.

34. Ogawa, "The Effects of Karaoke," 49–51.

35. Ogawa, "The Effects of Karaoke," 49.

36. Larry Gross, "Art and Artists on the Margins," in *On the Margins of Art Worlds*, ed. Larry Gross (Boulder, Colo.: Westview, 1995), 2.

37. James W. Carey, "A Cultural Approach to Communication," in *Communication and Culture* (Winchester, Mass.: Unwin Hyman, 1989).

38. For critiques of the identification of popular culture with lack of originality, see Herbert J. Gans, *Popular Culture and High Culture* (New York: Basic, 1974), 20–23; and Richard Shusterman, *Pragmatic Aesthetics: Living Beauty, Rethinking Art* (Malden, Mass.: Blackwell, 1991), 188–89.

39. Cohen, *Rock Culture*, 184.

40. Simon Frith, *Performing Rites: On the Value of Popular Music* (Cambridge, Mass.: Harvard University Press, 1996), 69. See also Weinstein, "History of Rock's Pasts," 142.

41. Johan Fornas, "Karaoke: Subjectivity, Play, and Interactive Media," *Nordicom Review* 1 (1994): 95.

42. Renee Graham, "'Psycho' Goes Down the Drain," *Boston Globe*, 5 December 1998, sec. C, p. 1; Cathy Horyn, "The Pace Is Ferocious, and Logic Elusive," *New York Times*, 2 March 1999, sec. B, p. 8.

43. Lenny Stoute, "Curtains for Clintons: Breeding Ground for New Talent Switches to Karaoke Format," *Toronto Star*, 7 December 1995, sec. H, p. 7. On antitechnology biases in music criticism, see Frith, "Art versus Technology."

44. Frith, *Performing Rites*, 169.

45. Deborah Wong, "'I Want the Microphone': Mass Mediation and Agency in Asian-American Popular Music," *Drama Review* 38 (1994).

46. Casey M. K. Lum, *In Search of a Voice: Karaoke and the Construction of Identity in Chinese America* (Mahwah, N.J.: Lawrence Erlbaum, 1995).

47. Frith, *Performing Rites*, 237.

48. Fornas, "Karaoke," 96.

49. On drag performance, see David Roman, "'It's My Party and I'll Die If I Want To!': Gay Men, AIDS, and the Circulation of Camp in U.S. Theatre," *Theatre Journal* 44 (1992). On star impersonators, see Lynn Spigel, "Communicating with the Dead: Elvis as Medium," *Camera Obscura* 23 (1990); and John Fiske, "Elvis: A Body of Controversy," in *Power Plays Power Works* (New York: Verso,

1993). On cover bands, see H. Stith Bennett, *On Becoming a Rock Musician* (Amherst: University of Massachusetts Press, 1993); Stephen B. Groce, "Occupational Rhetoric and Ideology: A Comparison of Copy and Original Music Performers," *Qualitative Sociology* 12 (1989); Susan Orlean, "Lounging," in *Saturday Night* (New York: Knopf, 1990).

50. Weinstein, "History of Rock's Pasts," 146. See also Karen Kelly, "Keeping Time," in *Stars Don't Stand Still in the Sky: Music and Myth*, ed. Karen Kelly and Evelyn McDonnell (New York: New York University Press, 1999); and Michael Bérubé, "The 'Elvis Costello Problem' in Teaching Popular Culture," *Chronicle of Higher Education* 13 (August 1999).

51. For good reviews, see Joli Jensen and John J. Pauly, "Imagining the Audience: Losses and Gains in Cultural Studies," in *Cultural Studies in Question*, ed. Marjorie Ferguson and Peter Golding (Thousand Oaks, Calif.: Sage, 1997); and Patrick Murphy, "Media Cultural Studies' Uncomfortable Embrace of Ethnography," *Journal of Communication Inquiry*, 23 (1999).

52. Janice A. Radway, "Reception Study: Ethnography and the Problems of Dispersed Audiences and Nomadic Subjects," *Cultural Studies* 2 (1988): 366. See also Ien Ang, "Ethnography and Radical Contextualism in Audience Studies," in *The Audience and Its Landscape*, ed. James Hay, Lawrence Grossberg, and Ellen Wartella (Boulder, Colo.: Westview, 1995); and Virginia Nightingale, *Studying Audiences: The Shock of the Real* (New York: Routledge, 1996).

53. Martin Allor, "Relocating the Site of the Audience," *Critical Studies in Mass Communication*, 5 (1988); John Erni, "Where Is the 'Audience'? Discerning the (Impossible) Subject," *Journal of Communication Inquiry* 13 (1989); Briankle G. Chang, "Deconstructing the Audience: Who Are They and What Do We Know about Them," in *Communication Yearbook 10*, ed. Margaret L. McLaughlin (Newbury Park, Calif.: Sage, 1987).

54. Nightingale, *Studying Audiences*, 95.

55. Robert Wuthnow, *Loose Connections: Joining Together in America's Fragmented Communities* (Cambridge, Mass.: Harvard University Press, 1998).

56. Lofland and Lofland, *Analyzing Social Settings*, 36.

57. John Van Maanen, *Tales of the Field: On Writing Ethnography* (Chicago: University of Chicago Press, 1988), 39 n.

58. Laurel Richardson, "Writing: A Method of Inquiry," in *The Handbook of Qualitative Research*, ed. Norman K. Denzin and Yvonna S. Lincoln (Thousand Oaks, Calif.: Sage, 1994), 516.

59. Jensen and Pauly, "Imagining the Audience," 167.

60. Herbert W. Simons, "In Praise of Muddleheaded Anecdotalism," *Western Journal of Speech Communication* 42 (1978): 23.

61. Henry Jenkins, Tara McPherson, and Jane Shattuc, "The Culture That Sticks to Your Skin: A Manifesto for a New Cultural Studies," in *Hop on Pop: The*

Pleasures and Politics of Popular Culture, ed. Henry Jenkins, Tara McPherson, and Jane Shattuc (Durham, N.C.: Duke University Press, forthcoming).

62. Lawrence Grossberg, "Is There Rock after Punk?" *Critical Studies in Mass Communication* 3 (1986); Susan McClary and Robert Walser, "Start Making Sense: Musicology Wrestles with Rock," in *On Record: Rock, Pop, and the Written Word*, ed. Simon Frith and Andrew Goodwin (New York: Pantheon, 1990).

63. Nick Hornby, *High Fidelity* (New York: Riverhead, 1995); Roddy Doyle, *The Commitments* (New York: Random House, 1989).

64. Tania Modleski, introduction to *Studies in Entertainment: Critical Approaches to Mass Culture* (Bloomington: Indiana University Press, 1986), xi.

65. Renato Rosaldo, *Culture and Truth* (Boston: Beacon, 1989), 103. Also see Carolyn Ellis and Michael G. Flaherty, "An Agenda for the Interpretation of Lived Experience," in *Investigating Subjectivity: Research on Lived Experience*, ed. Carolyn Ellis and Michael G. Flaherty (Newbury Park, Calif.: Sage, 1992), 4.

66. Jenkins, McPherson, and Shattuc, "Culture That Sticks to Your Skin."

67. George E. Marcus, "What Comes (Just) after 'Post'? The Case of Ethnography," in *Handbook of Qualitative Research*, 567.

Chapter 2

1. John Blacking, *How Musical Is Man?* (Seattle: University of Washington Press, 1973), 7; Dick Hebdige, *Subculture: The Meaning of Style* (London: Routledge, 1979), 112.

2. Henry Kingsbury, *Music, Talent, and Performance: A Conservatory Cultural System* (Philadelphia: Temple University Press, 1988), 59–83.

3. Erving Goffman, "On Face-Work," in *Interaction Ritual: Essays in Face-to-Face Behavior* (New York: Pantheon, 1967), 6.

4. Kingsbury, *Music, Talent, and Performance*, 5.

5. Goffman, "On Face-Work," 11.

6. Steve Jones, *Rock Formation: Music, Technology, and Mass Communication* (Newbury Park, Calif.: Sage, 1992), 51.

7. Bennett, *On Becoming a Rock Musician*, 154.

8. Bennett, *On Becoming a Rock Musician*, 155.

9. Jones, *Rock Formation*, 38–47.

10. Van Christy, *Foundations in Singing* (Dubuque, Iowa: William C. Brown, 1973), 3.

11. Dell Hymes, *Foundations in Sociolinguistics* (Philadelphia: University of Pennsylvania Press, 1974), 4–5.

12. Simon Frith, *Sound Effects: Youth, Leisure, and the Politics of Rock 'n' Roll* (New York: Pantheon, 1981), 35.

13. McClary and Walser, "Start Making Sense," 281–82.

14. Robert Rushmore, *The Singing Voice* (New York: Dembner, 1984), 156.

15. Frith, *Sound Effects*, 14–15.

16. On pop and rock musicians' lack of formal training, see Bennett, *On Becoming a Rock Musician*, 3; and Ruth Finnegan, *The Hidden Musicians: Music-Making in an English Town* (New York: Cambridge University Press, 1989), 133–42.

17. Frith, *Sound Effects*, 15.

18. Goffman, "On Face-Work," 19–23.

19. Michael Osborn and Suzanne Osborn, *Public Speaking*, 3d ed. (Boston: Houghton Mifflin, 1994), 49 (italics in original).

20. Orrin Klapp, "The Fool As a Social Type," *American Journal of Sociology* 55 (1950): 161.

21. Barbara Babcock, "Arrange Me into Disorder: Fragments and Reflections on Ritual Clowning," in *Rite, Drama, Festival, Spectacle: Rehearsals toward a Theory of Cultural Performance*, ed. John J. MacAloon (Philadelphia: Institute for the Study of Human Issues, 1984), 107.

Chapter 3

1. Greil Marcus, *Dead Elvis: A Chronicle of a Cultural Obsession* (New York: Doubleday, 1991), 29; Gilbert Rodman, *Elvis after Elvis: The Posthumous Career of a Living Legend* (New York: Routledge, 1996), 78–80.

2. Dwight Conquergood, "Communication as Performance: Dramaturgical Dimensions of Everyday Life," in *The Jensen Lectures: Contemporary Communication Studies*, ed. John I. Sisco (Tampa, Fla.: University of South Florida, 1982), 24–25.

3. Elizabeth C. Fine and Jean Haskell Speer, "A New Look at Performance," *Communication Monographs* 44 (1977): 374.

4. Richard Schechner, *Between Theater and Anthropology* (Philadelphia: University of Pennsylvania Press, 1985), 36.

5. Elizabeth C. Fine and Jean Haskell Speer, introduction to *Performance, Culture, and Identity*, ed. Elizabeth C. Fine and Jean Haskell Speer (Westport, Conn.: Praeger, 1992), 8–9.

6. Fine and Speer, introduction, *Performance, Culture, and Identity*, 10.

7. On lesbians and country music, see Rosa Ainley and Sarah Cooper, "She Thinks I Still Care: Lesbians and Country Music," in *The Good, the Bad, and the Gorgeous: Popular Culture's Romance with Lesbianism*, ed. Diane Hamer and Belinda Budge (San Francisco: HarperCollins, 1994); and B. Ruby Rich, "Standing by Your Girl," *Artforum* (summer 1992). On white teenagers and rap, see Mark Costello and David Foster Wallace, *Signifying Rappers: Rap and Race in the*

Urban Present (New York: Ecco Press, 1990); and Danny Hoch, "Flip," in *Jails, Hospitals and Hip-Hop* (New York: Villard, 1998), 17–22.

8. Ainley and Cooper, "She Thinks I Still Care," 52.

9. Douglas Coupland, *Generation X: Tales for an Accelerated Culture* (New York: St. Martin's, 1991); Neil Howe and Bill Strauss, *13th Gen: Abort, Retry, Ignore, Fail?* (New York: Random House, 1993).

10. Howe and Strauss, *13th Gen*, 52.

11. Richard Sennett, *The Fall of Public Man* (New York: Random House, 1978); Christopher Lasch, *The Culture of Narcissism* (New York: Norton, 1979).

12. Goffman, *Frame Analysis*, 359–66.

13. Howe and Strauss, *13th Gen*, 155.

14. Quoted in Howe and Strauss, *13th Gen*, 13.

15. Spigel, "Communicating with the Dead."

16. Clifford Geertz, "Deep Play: Notes on the Balinese Cockfight," in *The Interpretation of Cultures* (New York: Basic, 1973).

17. Basil Bernstein, "Social Class, Language, and Socialization," in *Class, Codes and Control*, vol. 1 (London: Routledge, 1971).

18. Sally F. Moore and Barbara G. Myerhoff, introduction to *Secular Ritual*, ed. Sally F. Moore and Barbara G. Myerhoff (Amsterdam: Van Gorcum, Assen, 1977), 3.

19. Conquergood, "Communication as Performance," 37.

20. Goffman, *Frame Analysis*, 269.

21. Cohen, *Rock Culture*, 154.

22. "Who Do You Sound Like?" 11 March 1997, <http://www.joltforum. com/jolt?14@39.ZvbFadHprmx^4@.ee6bce6/0> [accessed 29 May 1997].

23. Schechner, *Between Theater and Anthropology*, 124.

24. Conquergood, "Communication as Performance," 37.

25. Ronald J. Pelias, *Performance Studies: The Interpretation of Aesthetic Texts* (New York: St. Martin's, 1992), 96–97.

26. Goffman, *Frame Analysis*, 345–77.

27. Judith Butler, *Gender Trouble: Feminism and the Subversion of Identity* (New York: Routledge, 1990).

28. Richard Bauman, *Verbal Art as Performance* (Prospect Heights, Ill.: Waveland, 1977).

29. McClary and Walser, "Start Making Sense," 288.

Chapter 4

1. "It's Time to Maim That Tune," *Newsweek*, 29 June 1992, 57.

2. Ray Oldenburg, *The Great Good Place* (New York: Paragon, 1989); and Robert D. Putnam, "Bowling Alone: America's Declining Social Capital," *Journal of Democracy* (1995).

3. Putnam, "Bowling Alone," 76–77. Also see Gary Gumpert, *Talking Tombstones and Other Tales of the Media Age* (New York: Oxford University Press, 1987), 178. For a critique of this brand of media scapegoating and of the liberal angst about public life popularized by Putnam and others, see Michael Shapiro, "Bowling Blind: Post-Liberal Civic Society and the Worlds of Neo-Tocquevillean Social Theory," *Theory and Event* 1 (1997).

4. Richard Sennett, *The Fall of Public Man* (New York: Random House, 1978); Malcolm R. Parks, "Ideology in Interpersonal Communication: Off the Couch and into the World," in *Communication Yearbook 5*, ed. Michael Burgoon (New Brunswick, N.J.: Transaction Books, 1982); Eric M. Eisenberg, "Jamming: Transcendence through Organizing," *Communication Research* 17 (1990).

5. Sennett, *Fall of Public Man*, 3–4.

6. Daniel Boorstin, "From Traveler to Tourist: The Lost Art of Travel," in *The Image: A Guide to Pseudo-Events in America* (New York: Atheneum, 1961).

7. Mark Neumann, "The Trail Through Experience: Finding Self in the Recollection of Travel," in *Investigating Subjectivity: Research on Lived Experience*, ed. Carolyn Ellis and Michael G. Flaherty (Newbury Park, Calif.: Sage, 1992); Erik Cohen, "The Study of Touristic Images of Native People: Mitigating the Stereotype of a Stereotype," in *Tourism Research: Critiques and Challenges*, ed. Douglas G. Pearce and Richard W. Butler (New York: Routledge, 1993).

8. Erving Goffman, *Encounters: Two Studies in the Sociology of Interaction* (Indianapolis: Bobbs-Merrill, 1961), 61.

9. Cf. Edward M. Bruner, "Of Cannibals, Tourists, and Ethnographers," *Cultural Anthropology* 4 (1989).

10. Georg Simmel, "The Stranger," in *On Individuality and Social Forms* (Chicago: University of Chicago Press, 1971), 145.

11. Bruner, "Of Cannibals, Tourists, and Ethnographers," 441.

12. There is some evidence that a touristic stance toward karaoke is particularly common among young, affluent customers, particularly college students, and that this sometimes leads to tensions with karaoke's older, working- and middle-class supporters. See Vincent Doyle's nice paper, "Being Apart Together: Integration and Difference in a Karaoke Scene," presented at the annual meeting of the International Communication Association, San Francisco, May 1999; and Julia Chaplin, "Once More, with Irony," *New York Times*, 5 July 1998. Yet I've seen too many college kids become hopelessly devoted to karaoke (and working-class kids maintain an ironic detachment from it) to draw any hard and fast conclusions.

13. Boorstin, "From Traveler to Tourist," 98.

14. Erving Goffman, *The Presentation of Self in Everyday Life* (New York: Doubleday, 1959), 77–105.

15. Goffman, *Presentation of Self*, 78.

16. Jennifer Mandelbaum, "Couples Sharing Stories," *Communication Quarterly* 35 (1987).

17. Paul Watzlawick, Janet H. Beavin, and Don D. Jackson, *Pragmatics of Human Communication* (New York: Norton, 1967), 52.

18. Leslie A. Baxter and William W. Wilmot, "'Secret Tests': Social Strategies for Acquiring Information about the State of the Relationship," *Human Communication Research* 11 (1984): 184. Also see Erving Goffman, "Tie Signs," in *Relations in Public* (New York: Basic, 1971).

19. Leslie A. Baxter, "The Social Side of Personal Relationships: A Dialectical Perspective," in *Social Context and Relationships*, ed. Steve Duck (Newbury Park, Calif.: Sage, 1993), 148.

20. Baxter, "The Social Side of Personal Relationships."

21. Goffman, "Tie Signs"; Peter Berger and Hansfried Kellner, "Marriage and the Construction of Reality," *Diogenes* 46 (1964); Leslie A. Baxter, "Symbols of Relationship Identity in Relationship Cultures," *Journal of Social and Personal Relationships* 4 (1987).

22. Robert Hopper, Mark L. Knapp, and Lorel Scott, "Couples' Personal Idioms," *Journal of Communication* 31 (1981): 26; Elliott Oring, "Dyadic Traditions," *Journal of Folklore Research* 21 (1984): 25–26.

23. Goffman, *Presentation of Self*, 48.

24. Cohen, *Rock Culture*, 34.

25. Jane Jacobs, *The Death and Life of American Cities* (New York: Random House, 1961), 56.

26. Eisenberg, "Jamming," 146–49.

27. David Halberstam, *Summer of '49* (New York: Morrow, 1989), 44.

28. Goffman, *Frame Analysis*, 508.

29. Goffman, *Frame Analysis*, 507.

30. Donald Horton and R. Richard Wohl, "Mass Communication and Para-Social Interaction: Observations on Intimacy at a Distance," *Psychiatry* 19 (1956). For a pop music example, see Simon Frith, "The Real Thing—Bruce Springsteen," in *Music for Pleasure: Essays in the Sociology of Pop* (New York: Routledge, 1988).

31. Andrew Goodwin, "Sample and Hold: Pop Music in the Digital Age of Reproduction," in *On Record: Rock, Pop, and the Written Word*, ed. Simon Frith and Andrew Goodwin (New York: Pantheon, 1990), 269.

32. Goffman, *Frame Analysis*, 124–55.

33. R. D. Laing, *The Politics of Experience* (New York: Pantheon, 1967).

34. Sherri Cavan, *Liquor License* (Chicago: Aldine, 1966), 180. On the stigma of the "public woman," see Elizabeth Wilson, *The Sphinx in the City* (Berkeley: University of California Press, 1992), 8; and Janet Wolff, "The Culture of Separate Spheres," in *Feminine Sentences: Essays on Women and Culture* (Berkeley: University of California Press, 1990), 22–23.

35. Toru Mitsui, "Genesis of Karaoke," 41–42; Shinobu Oku, "Karaoke and Middle-Aged and Older Women," in *Karaoke around the World*, 55–60; Yano, "Floating World of Karaoke," 7.

36. Arlie R. Hochschild, *The Managed Heart: Commercialization of Human Feeling* (Berkeley: University of California Press, 1983).

37. Mavis Bayton, "How Women Become Musicians," in *On Record: Rock, Pop, and the Written Word*, ed. Simon Frith and Andrew Goodwin (New York: Pantheon, 1990), 254.

38. Cf. Val Hamer's excellent paper on female karaoke singers in a northeast English town. "There is a perception amongst these women that karaoke offers them an opportunity to participate in a social event on equal terms, that there is less violence than in other pubs, and that their opportunity to be 'vocal' extended beyond the realm of singing." Hamer, "'Getting Vocal Down the Local': A Study of Women and Karaoke," paper presented at the annual meeting of the British Sociological Association, York, U.K., April 1997), 11.

Chapter 5

1. Hochschild, *Managed Heart*.

2. Hochschild, *Managed Heart*, 7–9; Anat Rafaeli and Robert I. Sutton, "Expression of Emotion as Part of the Work Role," *Academy of Management Review* 12 (1987): 26–28; Aviad E. Raz, "The Slanted Smile Factory: Emotion Management at Disneyland," *Studies in Symbolic Interaction* 21 (1997).

3. Jennifer Cherniss, "A Winning Karaoke Setting," in *Karaoke: The Bible*, ed. Thomas A. Gonda Jr. (Oakland, Calif.: G-Man Publishers, 1993), 113.

4. Robin Leidner, *Fast Food, Fast Talk: Service Work and the Routinization of Everyday Life* (Berkeley: University of California Press, 1993), 24–43.

5. Sally Harrison-Pepper, *Drawing a Circle in the Square* (Jackson, Miss.: University Press of Mississippi, 1990), xv; Richard Schechner, *Environmental Theater*, 2d ed. (New York: Applause, 1987), xxviii–xxxvi.

6. Sal Piro, *Creatures of the Night: The Rocky Horror Picture Show Experience* (Detroit: Stabur Press, 1990).

7. Jacques Werth, *High Probability Selling* (Dresher, Pa.: Abba Publishing, 1993), 34–50.

8. Goffman, *Presentation of Self*, 146.

9. Leidner, *Fast Food, Fast Talk*, 35–36.

10. The Project on Disney, "Working at the Rat," in *Inside the Mouse: Work and Play at Disney World* (Durham, N.C.: Duke University Press, 1995), 126; G. M. Hostage, "Quality Control in a Service Business," *Harvard Business Review* 53 (1975): 102.

11. Leidner, *Fast Food, Fast Talk*, 31.

12. Leidner, *Fast Food, Fast Talk*, 26.

13. Hochschild, *Managed Heart*, 91–95; Project on Disney, "Working at the Rat," 110–11.

14. Greg M. Smith, "Introduction: A Few Words about Interactivity," in *On a Silver Platter: CD-ROMs and the Promise of a New Technology*, ed. Greg M. Smith (New York: New York University Press, 1999), 7; Laura Miller, "www.claptrap.com," *New York Times*, 15 March 1998, sec. 7, p. 43.

15. Rafaeli and Sutton, "Expression of Emotion," 26; Project on Disney, "Working at the Rat," 136–37.

16. Gross, "Art and Artists," 6.

17. Hochschild, *Managed Heart*, 33.

18. Hochschild, *Managed Heart*, 25.

19. "Do All of the Worst Singers Want to Sing the Hardest Songs?" 20 January 1997, <http://www.joltforum.com/jolt?13@39.ZvbFadHprmx^9@.ee6b9d8> [accessed 24 January 1997].

20. Arlie R. Hochschild, "Emotion Work, Feeling Rules, and Social Structure," *American Journal of Sociology* 85 (1979): 562.

21. Cas Wouters, "The Sociology of Emotions and Flight Attendants: Hochschild's *Managed Heart*," *Theory, Culture and Society* 6 (1989): 98–102.

22. Hochschild, *Managed Heart*, 187.

23. Goffman, *Presentation of Self*, 21.

24. Henri Peretz, "Negotiating Clothing Identities on the Sales Floor," *Symbolic Interaction* 18 (1995); Debra Gimlin, "Pamela's Place: Power and Negotiation in the Hair Salon," *Gender and Society* 10 (1996).

25. Peretz, "Negotiating Clothing Identities," 23.

26. Peretz, "Negotiating Clothing Identities," 23.

27. Carolyn Ellis, "'I Hate My Voice': Coming to Terms with Minor Bodily Stigmas," *Sociological Quarterly* 39 (1998).

28. "Am I Up Next?" 10 February 1997, <http://www.joltforum.com/jolt?13@39.ZvbFadHprmx^24@.ee6bb05/10> [accessed 27 January 1999].

29. Gimlin, "Pamela's Place," 512–13.

30. Gimlin, "Pamela's Place," 518.

31. Mark L. Knapp and Mark E. Comadena, "Telling It Like It Isn't: A Review of Theory and Research on Deceptive Communication," *Human Communi-*

cation Research 5 (1979): 272–73; Dan H. O'Hair and Michael J. Cody, "Deception," in *The Dark Side of Interpersonal Communication*, ed. William Cupach and Brian Spitzberg (Hillsdale, N.J.: Lawrence Erlbaum, 1994), 186.

32. Erving Goffman, *Encounters: Two Studies in the Sociology of Interaction* (Indianapolis: Bobbs-Merrill, 1961), 48.

33. Goffman, *Encounters*, 50.

34. Goffman, *Encounters*, 52.

35. Goffman, *Encounters*, 93.

36. Goffman, *Presentation of Self*, 152.

37. Karl Weick, *The Social Psychology of Organizing* (Reading, Mass.: Addison-Wesley, 1969), 89.

38. Rafaeli and Sutton, "Expression of Emotion," 28.

39. Project on Disney, "Working at the Rat," 139.

40. Gross, "Art and Artists," 3.

41. Goffman, *Presentation of Self*, 151.

42. Peretz, "Negotiating Clothing Identities," 28.

43. Goffman, *Presentation of Self*, 40.

44. Nancy Chodorow, *The Reproduction of Mothering* (Berkeley: University of California Press, 1978), 36, quoted in Janice A. Radway, *Reading the Romance: Women, Patriarchy, and Popular Literature* (Chapel Hill: University of North Carolina Press, 1984), 94.

45. Radway, *Reading the Romance*, 97 (italics in original).

46. "Karaoke Burnout," 19 March 1998, <http://www.joltforum.com/jolt?13@39.ZvbFadHprmx^29@.ee6c671/14> [accessed 24 January 1999].

Chapter 6

1. Gross, "Art and Artists."

2. Greg Tutwiler, "Singing in the Sunshine," *Mobile Beat Magazine*, September 1999.

3. Tino Balio, "A Novelty Spawns Small Businesses," in *The American Film Industry*, rev. ed., ed. Tino Balio (Madison: University of Wisconsin Press, 1985), 18. Karaoke's future expansion will also depend on its evolving relationship with the recording industry, which deserves a brief explanation. Karaoke bars pay performance fees to music publishers and composers through organizations like AS-CAP and BMI, and karaoke software producers pay mechanical fees to publishers and composers for the rights to record and reproduce songs. Because the rights to the vast majority of songs that appear on karaoke menus are held, in part, by publishing subsidiaries of major recording companies such as Warner, Universal, EMI, and BMG, these companies benefit twice from karaoke. Such matters may

seem irrelevant to performers' experience of karaoke, but they aren't. It's hard to shake the feeling that, no less than the "indie" artists who record on the majors' boutique labels, karaoke performers carry on their quaint dramas of identity and resistance strictly by license of these companies. All it would take is for a couple of these behemoths to shrug and they could buy out the U.S. karaoke industry wholesale or wipe it out entirely. More likely, they will continue to leave the karaoke business to smaller fish and quietly collect royalties, as they have with programmed music producers like Muzak.

4. "Sizing Up Your Karaoke Library," *Karaoke Singer Magazine*, November 2000, 25–26.

5. Cf. Yano, "Floating World of Karaoke," 7–8.

6. Robert Taylor, "Karaoke with a Theme," *Mobile Beat Magazine*, May 1998, 100.

7. Quoted in Rodman, *Elvis after Elvis*, 73.

8. Don Cusic, "Karaoke: High Tech and the Folk Tradition," *Tennessee Folklore Society Bulletin* 55 (1991).

9. Andrés Martinez, *24/7: Living It Up and Doubling Down in the New Las Vegas* (New York: Villard, 1999), 289.

10. "Karaoke Dreams," 17 August 1998, <http://jolt.karaoke.com/jolt?13@145.5v6qabPLr3i^3@.ee6cfbc> [accessed 26 September 2000].

11. Gloria Steinem, *Marilyn* (New York: Plume, 1987), 138.

12. Jacques Attali, *Noise: The Political Economy of Music*, trans. Brian Massumi (Minneapolis: University of Minnesota Press, 1985).

13. Attali, *Noise*, 134.

14. Attali, *Noise*, 132.

15. Attali, *Noise*, 135.

16. Attali, *Noise*, 137.

17. Attali, *Noise*, 32.

18. Greil Marcus, "Real Life Rock Top Ten," *Village Voice*, 7 October 1986.

19. Attali, *Noise*, 141.

20. Elizabeth Bell, "Toward a Pleasure-Centered Economy: Wondering a Feminist Aesthetics of Performance," *Text and Performance Quarterly* 15 (1995): 112.

CREDITS

INDEX

ABOUT THE AUTHOR

Rob Drew teaches communication at Saginaw Valley State University in Michigan. His research interests include ethnography, popular music, and media audiences.

SILENT URNS